Andreas Barella

A LANGUAGE OF THE UNKNOWN.

INFLUENCE AND COMPOSITION IN THE WORK OF SAMUEL BECKETT

Anno 2019

First edition: Copyright ©1999 by Andreas Barella.
E-book: Copyright ©2014 by Andreas Barella.

This edition:
Copyright ©2019, Casa Editrice Ericlea
ISBN 978-88-96975-17-6

All rights reserved. No part of this book may be used or reproduced in any manner whatsoever without written permission except in the case of brief quotations embodied in critical articles and reviews. For information address Casa Editrice Ericlea, Via Andreoni 4, CH–6850 Mendrisio, Switzerland. E-mail: info@ericlea-editrice.com

Our books may be purchased for educational, business, or sales promotional use. For information, please write to info@ericlea-editrice.com.

Casa Editrice Ericlea
Via Andreoni 4
CH–6850 Mendrisio – Switzerland
Phone: +41 91 646 62 61
info@ericlea-editrice.com
www.ericlea-editrice.com

To both of us

TABLE OF CONTENTS

INTRODUCTION 9

PART I – "THE NOTHING TO EXPRESS" WHAT SHOULD BECKETT WRITE ABOUT? THE *UNKNOWN*

INTRODUCTION	19
PLATO	23
Epistle VII	23
Phaedrus	29
Ion	32
MYSTICISM	37
Bhagavad-Gita	39
Medieval Mystics: Meister Eckhart and "De Imitatione Christi"	45
Summary	60

PART II – "THE NOTHING WITH WHICH TO EXPRESS AND THE NOTHING FROM WHICH TO EXPRESS" DIRECT PHILOSOPHICAL INFLUENCES ON BECKETT

INTRODUCTION	65
DANTE ALIGHIERI	68
Dante's Epistola to Cangrande Della Scala	69
Dante's Superiority Over the Classics	83
Belacqua and "Colui che fece per viltà il gran rifiuto" (*Inf.*, iii, 59-60)"	87
GIAMBATTISTA VICO	97

The Tension Between Giambattista Vico and René Descartes	97
"Filosofia" and "Filologia": Vico's Way of Conceiving History	105
The Three Ages of Human Society: "L'Età degli Dei", "L'Età degli Eroi", "L'Età degli Uomini"	116
Poetry, Language, Myth	123
Human Beings and History	130

PART III – "THE OBLIGATION TO EXPRESS" BECKETT AND THE SEARCH FOR A SENSE

PROSE: THE TRILOGY	137
Molloy's and Moran's Mobility	138
Molloy and Three Kinds of Movement: Physical, Mental and Linguistic	139
Moran	154
Malone's Immobility	159
The Unnamable's Frustration	169
An Attempt to Give a Structure to the Trilogy	184
DRAMA: BECKETT'S ALLEGORY AND HIS USE OF THE ABSURD	190
Wolfgang Hildesheimer's "Absurde Theater"	191
Communication and Moments of Tension in *Endgame*	195
CONCLUSION	205
BIBLIOGRAPHY	209
Primary Sources	209
Secondary Sources	212
About the Author and Notes	*220*

INTRODUCTION

> Choose therefore which of the
> two you prefer us to call you,
> dishonest or divine.
>
> (*Ion*, 447)

Plato's conclusive dilemma to Ion opens this paper and will accompany us throughout it. How shall we consider Samuel Beckett? Is he a "dishonest man", who modifies and annihilates the rules that guide the creation of literature and, more seriously, those that allow the leading of a quiet life? Is he a man who has spent his existence trying to demonstrate the absurdity of life and of people? A writer who has renounced his authority on his works and on the ideas he expresses, and who distances himself from what he writes? Or is he a "divine man", who acts in conformity with what the god of poetry indicates to be right? Or, in other words, why are people still reading his books and going to theatres to watch his plays, although Beckett sometimes seems anxious to prevent them from doing it?

His work develops in both directions but closes on itself like a circle endlessly forming and destroying itself. "Beckett is a destroyer who adds to existence, who enriches it while undermining it," writes Emile Michel Cioran in "Encounter With Beckett". Beckett removes the objects (and the words that correspond to them) from the perspective in which they are usually considered, and tries to re-discover their force, which has been lost over centuries of constant standardisation. This loss of normal language usage gives rise to the confusion contained in his works, but from that confusion his characters bring to a more final state the different ways of carrying out their search. The Irish writer lessens rationality (often by means of rationality itself) in order to understand the irrational *unknown*. His usage of language is symptomatic: his characters rely both on words and do not trust them.¹ It seems as if thanks to the sounds words produce, Beckett tries to get back to the original creation.

Beckett is involved in his characters' quest; he searches with them and through them, because he is not able to get to the heart of what he is looking for, but only has an intuition of it.² This problem of not being able to understand plainly permeates Beckett's work and holds the interest of audiences and readers. Beckett's sensibility is frustrated by solutions which are never definitive but, at the same time, it is spurred on to deepen itself by seeking a more permanent form of gratification.

It is that mechanism that I intend to analyse in this dissertation. I will try to discover how Beckett carries out his research, what he is looking for, which hindrances he has to cope with, the reasons for, and results of, his struggle. My aim is not to give an exhaustive description and interpretation of Beckett's particular works, but to find some of the sources that nourish and link all of them. My dissertation attempts to overcome the common idea of Beckett as a destroyer and as an absurd author; annihilation and absurdity are *used* by Beckett but are not his ultimate purpose; he destroys because he hopes to find a solution among the ruins.

Although Beckett's work is full of philosophical, literary and spiritual references, it would be a mistake to consider it as an illustration of a particular philosophical, literary or spiritual theory. As Aldo Tagliaferri affirms:

> [l]'opera beckettiana non si lascia degradare ad illustrazione di un *dato di fatto* pre-stabilito da una filosofia, ma questa degradazione viene attuata, a nostro avviso, tanto da Adorno quanto da Blanchot che, invece di affrontare l'attualizzazione dalla quale muove Beckett, si accontentano di presupporre compiuta l'attualizzazione, e quindi nullificano l'acutissimo tentativo

compiuto da Beckett per catturare e coinvolgere la soggettività del lettore. L'intersoggettività richiesta dalla lettura di Beckett deve essere avallata come tale e non essere sfruttata a totale vantaggio di *un* soggetto. (158)

Tagliaferri claims that Beckett's work has not to be debased to an illustration of a pre-defined philosophical reality, and that it is necessary for the reader to *examine* Beckett's position. It is not enough to *notice* its advent. Beckett tries to involve readers and audiences, he tries to enlarge their consciousness, and this fact has to be borne in mind throughout. In Bersani's words: "[w]hat interests us is the agreement, among critics of quite different interests and levels of insight, of how *expressive* Beckett's work is."(13)

The aim of my dissertation is to clarify Beckett's processes of composition, in order to set a more objective and far-reaching basis for an interpretation of his work. This way of considering Beckett "from above" i.e. starting from the literary influence other authors have had on the Irish poet is, in my opinion, much more suitable than considering him "from below" i.e. trying to extrapolate general theories from Beckett's published works. The "from below" method interprets the symbols, images, gestures (and non-gestures) of Beckett's characters and, starting from these interpretations, tries to trace the development of a Beckettian theory of life and of the role that literature has in it. This method has produced interesting results in the area of study which concentrates on the so called Theatre of the Absurd. It has focused on the mechanisms used by Beckett in order to continuously deny and reconsider each statement (cf. *Endgame*); on the ways used by the Irish dramatist in order to lessen the consciousness of his characters by letting their movements become automatic (reaching the extreme result of *Quad*, where four dumb people pace the same square, each one following his particular course); and, finally, on the ways applied by Beckett to throw the audience-readers in a state of confusion and frustration, in that each and every landmark is constantly denied (e.g. the character of Godot in *Waiting for Godot*). What is missing in the "from below" method is a consideration of Beckett's full mastering of his work. In fact, the Irish writer can be considered one of the most intelligent and sophisticated authors of our century. His texts are cunningly built up; each sentence and nearly each word is the result of a synthesis of philosophic and literary readings and, all together, they form a complex network of hidden references and hidden meanings.[3] It is on these aspects that I intend to concentrate i.e. the influences other authors have had on Samuel Beckett's writing process.

I have divided my dissertation into three parts. The starting point for my subdivision has been the following statement, taken from Beckett's *Three Dialogues with Georges Duthuit*: "there is nothing to express, nothing with which to express, nothing from which to express, no power to express, no desire to express, together with the obligation to express." (*Disjecta*, 139)

In Part One, I have concentrated on Beckett's "nothing to express" . What is this "nothing" made of? Where does it come from? Which forces push Beckett to write? Why is Beckett obliged to express himself? Why does he feel this duty? And why does he claim that expression is condemned to failure? Part I seeks to describe this "nothing" i.e. those aspects of Beckett's work which can be classified with the term *unknown*.

The first chapter concentrates on Plato. I will focus on *Epistle VII* in order to consider Plato's five levels of understanding; then I will examine *Phaedrus* (and the idea that a text is a means to attain a goal i.e. that of knowledge), and *Ion* (considering the foundation of poetry and the force that moves poets). The second chapter of Part I concentrates on mysticism. The first part of the chapter tries to clarify and develop the concepts described in the section about Plato with the help of spiritual texts, and to show how widely they can be applied to Beckett's works; the second part is concerned with

Introduction

Beckett's possible use of a negative mysticism, and will concentrate mainly on Meister Eckhart and on the *De Imitatione Christi*.

The second part of my dissertation is concerned with the "nothing with which to express" and with "the nothing from which to express". I have considered the direct philosophical influences of two authors on Beckett.

The first author is Dante Alighieri. I have analysed Dante's literary theories and his cosmology, which have been condensed and elaborated by Beckett. The aim of this comparison is that of showing how both Dante's and Beckett's poetry are an attempt to create a new way of expression (and, consequently, a new reality), Dante creating a new language (the Italian ideolect), and Beckett, destroying grammatical, syntactic, lexical rules and meaning and creating a sort of non-language (or rather, a way of expression which is to a certain extent not subject to conventional rules). Making reference to Dante's *Epistola XIII* to Cangrande della Scala, I have analysed those elements that, according to Dante, have to be considered before reading a doctrinal work, and I have applied them to Beckett's work. I have shown how Beckett's works produce a result on several levels at the same time (literal, allegorical, moral, anagogic). I have then considered the episode of Belacqua (*Purgatorio*, iv) and that of the Ante-Inferno (*Inferno*, iii).

The second chapter of Part II is devoted to Giambattista Vico. A first introductory part concentrates on the polemics between Vico and Descartes. On the one hand Descartes claims that history cannot be considered a subject for the scientific world, on the other Vico affirms that it is possible to make a science out of it. In his view history is a human product, and thus scientifically shows the evolution of human beings and of society. Many important Vichian topics are present in Beckett's works e.g. the limits of human beings in the comprehension of Nature, expressed in the "verum-factum" theory, or the fact that the historic and social worlds have been created by humans. Even Vico's theoretical scheme has been reconsidered by Beckett. Vico wanted to bring together Plato (theoretician of the existence of a universal knowledge which operates in humans, spur to Beckett's obligation to express), and Tacitus (who is not concerned with ideal human beings, but considers them as they are, cf. Beckett's characters) by means of philology in order to create what Vico, quoting Bacon, calls "l'universal repubblica delle lettere" (notice the similarity with the monologues spoken by Molloy and Moran in *Molloy*). Less obvious but even more interesting are the influences of ideas like that of the presence in humans of fundamental qualities (theorised by Plato) and developed by Vico with the name of "idea eterna"; the subdivision of history into three ages, theocratic, heroic and civilised; the consideration of language, poetry and myth as instruments of extreme importance in the development of human beings and societies; the existence of an ideal project towards which human beings tend with their behaviour. These themes have often been revised in a negative way by Beckett, especially in the trilogy *Molloy, Malone Dies, The Unnamable*.

Part III is the direct consequence of the two preceding ones. It applies the theoretical results I have achieved to the actual writings of the Author of *Waiting for Godot*. How does Beckett mix the various parts that compose the *unknown*, in order to look for a sense? In Part III we will see that Beckett develops his search in all possible directions. He never concentrates on a single aspect only, but is always aware of the presence of the others, and fuses them into a whole that tries to be omnipresent and omniscient.

I have devoted the first part to Beckett's prose. I have chosen to concentrate on *Molloy, Malone Dies* and *The Unnamable* because the trilogy is Beckett's longest work and it presents the widest treatment and development of the forces we are interested in. To analyse the trilogy, I have divided it according to the decreasing movement contained in it. The first chapter deals with Molloy's rambling and

Moran's journey to Ballybaba, what causes these movements, what they consist of, why they stop. The second chapter is concerned with Malone's loss of mobility, the changes he has to cope with, how he presents what I have said about mobility. The last chapter deals with the unnamable (I prefer not to use a capital letter when naming him because it would give the impression of a name) and his frustration; his attempt to go silent and to detach himself from any form of movement.I have analysed Molloy's - apparently chaotic - circular movements (physical, mental and in language); Moran's difficulty in understanding spirituality and his gradual loss of instinct and rationality; Malone's being resigned to the immortality of the tension which has immobilised him and which has arisen from the confrontation of his rationality with his spirituality; and finally the unnamable's standstill. The unnamable is already detached from instinct, rationality, language, but is not yet absorbed by the force he recognises as being the only one which absorbs all his interest.

A second part is concerned with drama. In this chapter, I look at how the tension, still unresolved at the end of the trilogy, has been developed in Beckett's plays. I start by concentrating on Beckett's (non-)usage of allegorical actions and on his creating works that have been defined as "absurd". In the introduction to this chapter I have analysed and tried to set out some ideas found in Wolfgang Hildesheimer's article "Über das absurde Theater". I then concentrate on *Endgame* and on the tension that arises during the performance of the play.

Deirdre Bair in her *Biography* writes that "[i]t [*The Unnamable*] is one of his [Beckett's] two favourite works and like the other, *Endgame*, it is one which gives him enormous personal satisfaction." (425) It is thus on these two works that I concentrate most in order to draw some general conclusions about Samuel Beckett's work.

PART I – "THE NOTHING TO EXPRESS"

WHAT SHOULD BECKETT WRITE ABOUT? THE *UNKNOWN*

INTRODUCTION

> I'm no intellectual. All I am is feeling.
> (Interview with Gabriel
> D'Aubarède, 1961)

Dante Alighieri in his *Epistola* to Cangrande della Scala writes: "Volentes igitur aliqualem notitiam tradere de parte operis alicuius, oportet aliquam notitiam tradere de toto cuius est pars." (608) It is necessary, Dante claims, to give some information about a work as a whole before explaining a particular part of it.

This is the aim of Part I. It seeks to describe those aspects of Beckett's work which can be described as belonging to the *unknown*. If something is unknown, it means that neither its name, nor its nature, nor its origins are known. Beckett's readers and those people who have seen one of his plays, are certainly familiar with that feeling of dissatisfaction, of not being able to understand why such a simple text has impressed them so much. They try to connect their feelings with a verbal description but fail; they try to describe what the text is about but are not totally able to do so; they try to understand where their dissatisfaction springs from but are disappointed at not finding any solution.

The *unknown* does not only disappoint Beckett's readers and audiences, the Writer himself is obsessed with it. Beckett deals with it in nearly every work and was confronted with its force all his life long. But why, if the *unknown* was so important for Beckett, did he not give a definition to it? Would it have been too difficult? Did he consciously refuse to do it? Other questions are puzzling. Is the *unknown* a negative or a positive force? Where does it come from? To what extent does Beckett refer to it in his work? These questions must be carefully considered before starting an interpretation of

Part I – "The Nothing to express"

individual texts by Beckett.

It is certainly true that Beckett's work is based on negation, silence, failure, but not only, and not only as negation has it been perceived by audiences and readers. The hope Vaclav Havel wrote about is a hint of the potential presence of a positive meaning in Beckett. The fact that the positive will not be developed and will be frustrated, does not mean that it is not present and that the reader-spectator does not perceive its force.

Part I is an introduction to what I think makes Samuel Beckett one of the greatest writers of the twentieth century; it is a survey of those mechanisms and forces that made, and still make, him stand out as a man of genius.

In the two following chapters I will try to name, to give a definition to, and to explain what Giovanni Cattanei calls "la situazione drammatica fondamentale" (188), the basic dramatic situation. Considering the vagueness of the concepts of *unknown* and of "basic dramatic situation", I will not, in Part I, present my point of view simply with evidence taken from Beckett's works, but I will try to define these concepts by means of parallelisms with similar forces contained in texts which already have a place in history.[4] This parallelism should enable a first comprehensive view of Beckett's work to be made.

Beckett himself claimed that he was looking for a new means of expression which could cope with a material nobody had tried to accommodate before. Let us consider what Beckett said in an interview with Tom Driver:

> "The confusion is not my invention. We cannot listen to a conversation for five minutes without being acutely aware of the confusion. It is all around us and our only chance now is to open our eyes and see the mess. It is not a mess you can make sense of." [...]
> Then [Beckett] began to speak about the tension in

art between the mess and form. Until recently, art has withstood the pressure of chaotic things. It has held them at bay. It realized that to admit them was to jeopardize form. "How could the mess be admitted, because it appears to be the very opposite of form and therefore destructive of the very thing that art holds itself to be?" But now we can keep it out no longer, because we have come into a time when "it invades our experience at every moment. It is there and it must be allowed in."

I [Tom Driver] granted this might be so, but found the result to be even more attention to form than was the case previously. And why not? How, I asked, could chaos be admitted to chaos? Would not that be the end of thinking and the end of art? If we look at recent art we find it preoccupied with form. Beckett's own work is an example. Plays more highly formalized than *Waiting for Godot*, *Endgame*, and *Krapp's Last Tape* would be hard to find.

"What I am saying does not mean that there will henceforth be no more form in art. It only means that there will be new form, and that this form will be of such a type that it admits the chaos and does not try to say that the chaos is really something else. The form and the chaos remain separate. The latter is not reduced to the former. That is why the form itself becomes a preoccupation, because it exists as a problem separate from the material it accommodates. To find a form that accommodates the mess, that is the task of the artist now. [...] With classical art, all is settled. But it is different at Chartres. There is the unexplainable, and there art raises questions that it does not attempt to answer." (Driver, 218-20, emphasis added)

Beckett admits both the need for a form and the unavoidable presence of chaos, and he claims that these two have to find a new, still unexplainable, way of expression because chaos will never become pure form, nor will form be able to accommodate chaos. Chaos is a state of complete and thorough disorder and confusion, and escapes from what our rational mind can understand because it is too wide. It is in this direction i.e. the attempt to cope with chaos by means of (new) forms that we will proceed to examine.

In Part II and III we will see how Beckett builds and tries to understand his own unexplainable Chartres; in Part I we will visit the cathedral to see it ourselves and make up our mind upon what it could possibly be made of.

The chapter about Plato deals mainly with the origin of what Beckett called "chaos" or "mess" and I will call the *unknown*; and the chapter about mysticism deals with Beckett's direct relationship with it: the *unknown* is still unexplainable, but it becomes something real.

PLATO

Samuel Beckett read Plato, together with the Gnostics, Aretino and Aristotle on the Greek philosopher Thales while he was living in London in 1932 (Knowlson, 161). Plato's view of art is notoriously rather negative. His conclusions are that art (and poetry is a part of it) does not show Truth; that art does not improve man because it is untruthful; that it is not educational because it is directed to the worst part of man's soul i. e. the irrational. Plato's aim, with the help of his theory, is to subject art to philosophy because only in this way could art lead to Truth. Art for its own sake is of no use.

This debate on the dependence of art on philosophy is strongly present in Plato's *Epistle VII*, in *Phaedrus*, and in *Ion*. We have to bear this in mind when dealing with these works, although the purposes of this chapter differ slightly from Plato's. He wanted art to serve philosophy. The first sub-chapter, with thanks to Plato, sketches a definition of art as a philosophical creation: love of knowledge which creates the form of art that interests us i.e. poetry.

The second part of this chapter applies to Beckett's works some concepts taken from *Phaedrus*; and the third, based on *Ion*, deals with the force that moves poets.

Epistle VII

As stated in *Epistle VII* (533-5), the search for understanding proceeds on five levels: the first one is the name, the second is the definition, the third is the image, the fourth is knowledge (the knowledge of the object), and the fifth is the object itself.

None of these levels seems to be applied by Beckett. He cannot name the object of his search, consequently he cannot define it nor describe it by means of a physical image.⁵ He has no knowledge of the object, he does not know it. Thus he cannot possess it. Plato affirms that

> [f]ourth comes *knowledge* and intelligence and true opinion regarding these objects; and these we must assume to form a single whole, which does not exist in vocal utterance or in bodily forms but in souls. (535)

The object cannot be possessed, Plato claims; its essence must form itself in souls. This is the reason why knowledge is much more important than the name, the definition and the image. Beckett is frequently concerned with these concepts. The widely-quoted extract from *Three Dialogues*:

> that there is nothing to express, nothing with which to express, nothing from which to express, no power to express, no desire to express, together with the obligation to express" (*Disjecta*, 139),

is a sort of paraphrase of Plato's statement. The first three platonic concepts are negated: "nothing with which to express" describe the invalidity of words, "nothing from which to express", and "no power to express" show that research is groundless, that each definition is senseless because an exact statement on the meaning, nature or limits of a word is impossible. The remaining clauses seem contradictory: "there is nothing to express, [...] no desire to express, together with the obligation to express." The first statement could be used to demonstrate that the fourth and the fifth level of Plato's method of research are useless: if there is nothing to express, it is impossible to know it (with "it" I mean Beckett's "nothing" i.e. the *unknown*) nor to possess it in its essence. But Plato also claims the same thing: "a whole [...] which does not exist in vocal utterance or in bodily forms". There is nothing to express in that the rational part of man has no control over the knowledge of a particular object or idea. In other words, if we consider only the mind of man there is nothing to express, but if we consider his soul there is.[6] And, in fact, the two remaining statements affirm that there is something to be said, that Beckett is forced to give voice to something. In spite of his will (no desire to express), Beckett has to speak (the obligation to express). Although he does not want it, he has knowledge of something. It is a first allusion to the presence of a force which obliges Beckett to write. This force, which contrasts with Beckett's attitude towards writing, is the source of his inspiration. Beckett's negative statements have to be considered as a refusal of his rational part to pay heed to that force which operates in his soul and which compels him to write.

Notice that in MS 2907 of the Beckett International Foundation in Reading (a letter dating 9.3.1949, from Beckett to George Duthuit on Bram Van Velde, now in Mason, 1996), he adds:

> Partons cette fois-ci du rapport. C'est là où nous semblons nous rejoindre le mieux. Par rapport nous entendons, naturellement, non seulement celui, primaire, entre artiste et ce que le dehors lui propose, mais aussi et surtout ceux qui, en dedans de lui, lui assurent des lignes de fuite et de recul et des changements de tension et lui dispensent, entre autres bienfaits, celui de se sentir plusieurs (au bas mot), tout en restant (bien entendu) unique. Il peut donc se détourner du visible immédiat sans que cela tire à conséquences, sans cesser pour autant d'être un terme de relation. [...]
> Est-ce à dire qu'un Bram, se refusant (à supposer qu'il y soit pour quelque chose) au rapport primaire, tire forcément son expression du jeu des autres? [...] Et si c'est non, peut-on concevoir une expression en l'absence de

rapports quels qu'ils soient, aussi bien entre le moi et le non-moi qu'à l'intérieur de celui là?
Faut-il préciser la nature de ces rapports de soi en soi? Je suis mal placé pour le faire, n'en bénéficiant plus guère. Et je tendrai irrésistiblement à ramener au mien le cas de Bram, puisque c'est là la condition de puovoir y être et en parler, et puis pour d'autres raisons moins avouables. [...]
Ainsi térébré, pour parler comme Fénéon, l'artiste peut se rouler dans la peinture dite non figurative en toute tranquillité, avec l'assurance de n'être jamais à court de thèmes, d'être toujours devant lui-même et avec autant de variété que s'il n'avait jamais renoncé à flâner aux bords de la Seine. Et ici encore triomphe la définition de l'artiste comme celui qui ne cesse d'être *devant*. Au lieu d'être devant les précipitants il est devant les précipités. Tu parles d'une villégiature.
Pour moi la peinture de Bram ne doit rien à ces piètres consolations. Elle est nouvelle parce que la première à répudier le rapport sous toutes ces formes. <u>Ce n'est pas le rapport avec tel ou tel ordre de vis-à-vis qu'il refuse, mais l'état d'être en rapport tout court et sans plus, l'état d'être devant.</u> Il y a longtemps qu'on attend l'artiste assez courageux, assez à son aise dans les grandes tornades de l'intuition, pour saisir que la rupture avec le dehors entraîne la rurture avec le dedans, qu'aux rapports naïfs il n'existe pas de rapports de remplacement, que ce qu'on appelle le dehors et le dedans ne font qu'un. Je ne dis pas qu'il ne cherche pas à renouver. Ce qui importe, c'est qu'il n'y arrive pas. Sa peinture est, si tu veux, l'impossibilité de renouver. Il y a, si tu veux, refus et refus d'accepter son refus. C'est peut-être ce qui rend cette peinture possible. Pour ma part, c'est le *gran rifiuto*

qui m'intéresse, non pas les héroïques tortillements auxquels nous devons une chose si belle. J'en suis navré. Ce qui m'intéresse c'est l'au-delà du dehors-dedans où il fait son effort, non pas la portée de l'effort même. L'exilé béat n'habite pas Montrouge. [...] Que peint-il donc, avec tant de mal, s'il n'est plus devant rien? Dois-je vraiment essayer de le redire, en rafraîchissant les images? Quoi que je dise, j'aurai l'air de l'enfermer à nouveau dans une relation. Si je dis qu'il peint l'impossibilité de peindre, la privation de rapporter, d'objet, de sujet, j'ai l'air de le mettre en rapport avec cette impossibilité, avec cette privation, devant elles. Il est dedans, est-ce la même chose? Il les est, plutôt, et elles sont lui, d'une façon pleine, et peut-il y avoir des rapports dans l'indivisible? Pleine? Indivisible? Evidemment pas. Ça vit quand même. Mais dans une telle densité, c'est-à-dire simplicité, d'être, que seule l'éruption peut en avoir raison, y apporter le mouvement, en soulevant tout d'un bloc. [...] J'essaie seulement d'indiquer la possibilité d'une expression en dehors du système de rapports tenu jusqu'à présent pour indispensable à qui ne sait pas de contenter de son seul nombril. Si tu me demandes pourquoi la toile ne reste pas blanche, je peux seulement invoquer cet intelligible besoin, à tout jamais hors de cause, d'y foutre de la couleur, fût-ce en y vomissant son être. [...]
Finalement, pour reprendre un motif où je n'ai jamais su bien te suivre, je ne vois pas du tout comment un travail pareil peut accrocher des considérations sur le temps et l'espace, ni pourquoi, dans ces toiles qui nous font grâce de ces catégories, on serait tenu de les remettre, sous des espèces plus riantes que celles familières de la division, extensibilité, compressibilité,

mensurabilité, etc., à l'infini. On connaît déjà de ces honorables tentatives de bonification. Et dire que la peintre, en enduisant une toile de couleurs, s'engage nécessairement dans la voie des relations spatiales et temporales, me semble vrai uniquement pour celui qui n'a pas cessé de les faire intervenir sous la forme de rapports, ce qui n'est pas le cas de Bram, si j'ai bien bafouillé. [...] Que Bram fasse état de son passé, d'avenir meilleur et de Pietà à double vierge-mère, me laisse bien sûr froid comme Malone, c'est a dire à peine tiède, exception faite des extrémités, dont la tête. [...]
Je n'ai fait que dire la même chose que par deux fois déjà. Je ne peux plus écrire de façon suivie sur Bram ni sur n'importe quoi. Je ne peux pas écrire *sur*. Alors il va falloir, si tu n'es pas complètement dégoûté de moi, que tu ne poses des questions. J'essaierai d'y répondre. Mais sache que moi qui ne parle guère de moi ne parle guère que de ça. (Mason, 45-8, emphases added)

Beckett is looking for a new way of expression, but his search is impossible to be carried out if he applies the common rules of knowledge; he does not accept to being in front of an object and describe it, he is neither interested in the object itself nor in the relationship between himself and what he could describe. It is a lack of means of expression that Beckett describes, and Bram Van Velde's pictures demonstrate this lack. They are produced by a refusal to use whatsoever means of expression and by the necessity of giving a voice to the inmost part of the soul ("vomiter son être"). The dichotomy between the lack of means to express and the need to express, is constant in Beckett's works. The following chapter deals with the need to express, trying to define why Beckett has written, which force has pushed him to write, and what he is writing about.[7]

Phaedrus

Plato, almost at the end of *Phaedrus*, says that "in the written word there is necessarily much that is playful, and that no written discourse, whether in metre or in prose, deserves to be treated very seriously." (573) This speech is pronounced during a discussion about the greater clarity and fullness of orality compared with writing. Plato starts by saying that in a written text there is much that is playful, and that a text is never composed with too much seriousness. The lack of seriousness in Beckett's novels and plays is evident. His characters behave, act, speak, describe objects and tell stories in a comical way.[8] The trilogy's comical-type, for example, is that of negating the words that have already been pronounced. "The pale gloom of rainy days was better fitted to my taste, no, that's not it, to my humour, no, that's not it either, I had neither taste nor humour, I lost them early on." (*Molloy*, 29). Or by upsetting a sentence with a standardised meaning, as in the following example where the expected word should be "living". "I was on my way to my mother, whose charity kept me dying" (*Molloy*, 23; emphasis added).

Beckett uses these devices to depict his characters' confusion and their inability to take any decision (cf. Part III), but another reason can be extrapolated from Plato's words. Hiding Truth by means of comical elements helps to sort out readers; those who are satisfied with literal meaning (in Beckett's case, *frustrated* by literal meaning) are not spurred on to search for further values. The others, who think that there is something more to be discovered, accept the text's tricks and investigate further. A written text has to put some filters between the reader and the Truth it contains because that Truth has to be discovered and not given. This mechanism need not necessarily be conscious; Beckett wants to obstruct the force that has pushed him to write by mixing it with comical elements, and the result is that of selecting motivated readers. By investigating, the reader aims at being completely involved in the text from which will consequently "burst out the light of intelligence and reason" (*Epistle VII*, 541).

The text as a means of attaining a goal (that of knowledge) and not as an end in itself, is not only the conclusion of this first reasoning, but also the introduction to the second. Plato writes that "the best of them [discourses] really serve only to remind us of what we know". (*Phaedrus*, 573)

Texts are useful to the reader if they help his memory to recall higher concepts. Texts do not state the Truth, they hint at it. Where should readers have learned these Truths? Plato implies the existence of his Academy, where frequent and intense dialogue should light the spark of cognition. Beckett leads no academy, he can offer only his written texts and no other teaching. This means either that Beckett's works are self-sufficient (i.e. they clearly state the Truth they contain), or, if they contain Truth, that it will be difficult to discover it because no explanation is added to the text. The first possibility is unlikely because Beckett's novels and plays constantly reduce, with the purpose of annihilating, their semantic meaning.[9] If we accept the second possibility, we come back to the question stated some lines above. Where should Beckett's readers learn the Truth Beckett hints at in his texts? The answer is a demanding one; the reader has to be both student and teacher of his personal Academy, he has to interact with the book till the written words become alive; until from the printed text there emerges the voice of Truth. When the book teaches its lesson, the reader has reached a higher degree of consciousness, and vice versa.

The comprehension of Beckett's works is implicit, as is their composition. At first glance their Truth is hidden from the reader, as their writing was incomprehensible for Beckett. In *Molloy*, Beckett expresses this thought: "[n]ot to want to say, not to know what you want to say, not to be able to say what you think you want to say, and never to stop saying, or hardly ever, that is the thing to keep in mind, even in the heat of composition." (27) Molloy understands that he does not know the contents of what he is saying or will say, nor the reasons for his writing. That problem is important for Beckett. The Author of *Molloy* states that he does not know what Truth is, he is not in possession of the Truth he is dealing with in his works. So, how can we, the readers, look for it?[10] What shall we search for if the one who hides things has no idea of what he is hiding? I will try to give an answer in the sub-chapter about *Ion*. At this point the answer is still not relevant. What is important is that on Beckett's side the consequences of this problem have been that he has written. So the best action that the reader can perform is to *read* Beckett's works.

It could be argued that Plato's idea is in contradiction with what I have said about Beckett's lack of clarity. Plato claims that the best man is the one

> who thinks that only in words about justice and beauty and goodness spoken by teachers for the sake of instruction and really written in a soul is clearness and perfection and serious value (*Phaedrus*, 573)

Beckett is dealing with justice and beauty in that a part of his being is looking for Truth; it struggles to grasp Truth, whatever this might be (cf. Part I, Ch. 3. on mysticism). This is shown in the unnamable's last words: "you must go on, I can't go on, you must go on, I'll go on, you must say words, as long as there are any." (381) This Truth that Beckett has the perception of, is very difficult to describe; it is inside his soul but he is not able to translate it clearly into words (in Part I, Ch. 3. I will consider the relation Beckett-Truth). He has to go on saying "words as long as there are any", in order to tear aside the veil that, inside his soul, covers Truth. There is seriousness in Beckett's writings, Beckett is seriously in search of Truth.[11] His clearness and perfection are shown in his search, and not in his words.

Ion

Plato's aim, with his dialogues, is not to represent real talk, but to picture models of ideal conversations. The ideal talk, in *Ion*, is about the foundation of poetry. Socrates speaks with Ion, a famous rhapsodist and actor, and demonstrates that Ion's greatness stems from divine power, and not from any personal quality. Socrates says:

> For, as I was saying just now, this is not an art in you, whereby you speak well on Homer, but a divine power, which moves you like that in the stone which Euripides named a magnet, but most people call "Heraclea stone." (421)

Art is not inside men, Socrates claims, it comes from divine power. The poet is an instrument in the Muse's hands. He is able to compose poetry only when the god speaks to him.

> For a poet is a light and winged and sacred thing, and is unable ever to indite until he has been inspired and put out of his senses, and his mind is no longer in him: every man, whilst he retains possession of that, is powerless to indite a verse or chant an oracle. [...] And for this reason God takes away the mind of these men and uses them as his ministers, just as he does soothsayers and godly seers, in order that he we who hear them may know that it is not they who utter these words of great price, when they are out of their wits, but that it is God himself who speaks and addresses us through them. (423)

If the poet is not possessed by the god of poetry, if he is not "out of his senses", he will not be able to write a verse. This idea that it is not thanks to intellectual faculties that a person becomes a poet is of great help in the comprehension of Beckett's life and work.

We have already considered the passage taken from *Three Dialogues*. "No desire to express, together with the obligation to express", is a sentence which shows the division between Beckett's mind, which has no desire to express, and his spiritual part, where the god manifests himself, which is forced to express. Beckett is totally lacking in will power but nevertheless is compelled to express himself. He is possessed by the god but his intellect opposes it. On one side we have the inevitable process of creation, on the other we have Beckett's opposition. An example:

> A parrot, that's what they're up against, a parrot. If they had told me what I have to say, in order to meet with their approval, I'd be bound to say it, sooner or later. But God forbid, that would be too easy, my heart wouldn't be in it, I have to puke my heart out too, spew it up whole along with the rest of the vomit, it's then at last I'll look as if I mean what I'm saying, it won't be just idle words. (*The Unnamable*, 308)

"They" is the term the unnamable uses when referring to the Muse (cf. Part III, Ch. 1. on the unnamable, for a more detailed discussion of the meaning of "they"). The unnamable is reluctant to speak out of his heart, he only wants to say words invented by his mind. He is forced to speak, and in fact he does so, but, reporting his thoughts, he obstructs the Muse's voice by not allowing its development and expression.

Plato claims that poets are ministers of the god of poetry, and compares them to soothsayers and godly seers. The poet is a very important person, a "light and winged and sacred thing". Plato pays these compliments to poets because they are near to the god of poetry, near to the dispenser of Truth, and they report his voice, "these words of great price". There seems not to be any choice for the poet; he cannot refuse his task. Plato, at least, does not make reference to that problem. Ion, in fact, is happy to perform his art: reciting Homer is the only thing in his life that involves him completely. When giving a good recitation, Ion is in ecstasy; he really feels to be part of the scenes he is describing.

The difference between Ion and Beckett is that Beckett does not accept the role of man possessed by the Muse. He does not feel near the source of knowledge, he is not honoured at being an instrument of the Muse. Instead of a holy duty, Beckett sees that voice as a curse. His refusal is not enough, he still hears the Muse's voice and has to report it. The result of his way of accounting is shown in his annihilating style, cf. Part III. This duty to express is constant in his work.[12]

The affinity between Beckett and Ion, concerning the creation process, could be applied to many other writers. It acquires a particular importance in Beckett's work because the problem of not knowing how and why to write has become the work itself. Beckett, possessed by the god, speaks of the problems he encounters when having to bow to him. An Ion who recites a reciting Ion who is reciting a Ion who recites Ion, ad libitum.

Beckett himself is not able to explain what the god wants him to say. His reluctance to help readers (and actors and directors) to understand his works, show that the purport of his novels and plays cannot be explained with words, that it lies behind the actual written text and there it remains if the reader looks for an easy and exhaustive solution to his questions. "If I knew who Godot was, I would have said so in the play" said Beckett to Alan Schneider; and, to Harold Hobson, "If Godot were God, I would have called him that" (Deirdre Bair, 405-6).

Beckett never affirms that his works are a series of casual events or words. The carefulness of stage directions, and Beckett's extreme precision when attending rehearsals ("demanding, always demanding," said Jean Martin, Deirdre Bair, 419), show that he feels how the plays have to be performed in order to develop their full force.

The reader or the spectator must not focus his attention on a particular element of the novel or of the play. In order to overcome the barrier of Beckett's words, an interpretation has to pass through certain phases, because what the reader reads are words created by Beckett's refusal to write, together with his need to express, and are consequently contradictory and unclear. The first step is that the reader has to accept the god's guide and thus he has to surrender to Beckett's voice. It is of primary importance that the reader does not use his will-power to oppose the comprehension of the text; the literal meaning being nearly non-existent, he is obliged to concentrate on something else, i.e. the *unknown*. *Lessness* and its random composition are an extreme example: the reader has to concentrate on the pure sounds of words linked in a meaningless order, and among these sounds he has to discern the *unknown*.

The effort to direct his attention towards the *unknown*, and this is the second step, cannot be performed by the reader's mind because his intelligence is constantly frustrated. The *unknown* has to be felt inside the reader's heart, where it has to leave a strong and deep imprint. Plato claims that the reader is the last link in a "production of feelings" and the poet himself is the first, "but it is the god who through the whole series draws the souls of men whithersoever he pleases, making the power of one depend on the other." (427-9) Although Beckett's words do not cooperate with the god's force, they contain it. The reader is thus in direct contact with the god; he communicates with him in spite of Beckett's opposition.

Phase number three is the longest one; the reader has to be patient. He has to wait for the *unknown* to grow inside his soul and eventually manifest itself in a higher degree of consciousness. The result is that the subsequent reading is different from the previous one; the reader feels more acquainted with the text because his knowledge of the text's force has increased.

In other words, the reader has to let the god operate in his soul, he has to allow this process, because he cannot be fascinated by non-existent plots, non-existent dialogues, non-existing characters.[13] The reader's mind has to surrender to his soul. This does not mean that Beckett's works have to be intuitively interpreted; a rational explanation is the aim of every useful analysis, but the rationalisation of an interpretation of Beckett's works, so vague and contradictory, is never satisfying because it is inexhaustive. Beckett's words can be rationalised, but there still remains the voice of the Muse which cannot be tracked down. Beckett never commented on his books, and he avoided personal questions because he knew that each of his statements would have been used as a reading-key (of something he could not define, either). He kept silent so that his works, filled with his personal words, could hint at the Muse's whispering.

The god of poetry is speaking, Beckett does not understand it. The Irish writer's mind, his rational part, refuses to report a message it has not understood, but his spiritual part knows that the message is essential. Beckett has to educate people, but he does not know how to, nor what he has to teach.

MYSTICISM

This chapter deals with Samuel Beckett's direct relationship with the *unknown*. In the previous chapter we have often encountered a barrier to rational explanations of aspects of Beckett's work. It has been necessary to speak of Truth, spirituality, Muses, gods of poetry and poetical forces that operate on people. This terminology is as vague as the concepts it is concerned with, but is of an extreme importance for the understanding of Beckett's works. It is the quintessence of the *unknown* that pervades his novels and plays. Or, in other words, it is the universality added to Beckett's contemporary search, the spiritual part added to the intellectual one.

In Beckett's works we find many occasions that could be easily read in an esoteric way e.g. the constant presence of the letters "M" and "W" (Molloy, Moran, Malone, Murphy, Watt, Mercier, etc.) which recall the primordial Sanskrit sound OM. Even his language is often cryptic, as Tagliaferri notes.

> Entro certi limiti il linguaggio beckettiano mantiene le caratteristiche di quella lingua che, secondo Madame Blavatsky, gli antichi sacerdoti usavano per rivolgersi agli dèi; "essendo il suono il più potente ed il più efficace degli agenti magici e la prima delle chiavi che apre la porta di comunicazione fra i Mortali e gli Immortali," questo linguaggio era "composto di suoni e non di parole; di suoni, di numeri e di forme". Nella trilogia, naturalmente, la connotazione di queste immagini non è più teosofica, bensì critica. (127)

Tagliaferri claims that Beckett's language is, to a certain extent, similar to the language ancient priests use to communicate with gods.

Sounds, numbers and forms, Tagliaferri adds, are the most powerful magic spells. In Beckett, words tend to be creative e.g. the unnamable looks for a magic spell to get silent; Moran thinks Father Ambrose's words are magic because they consecrate communion. Beckett's works have thus to be considered in a musical and magic way too, but of course this interpretation has to be taken critically.

In an interview with Beckett, Tom Driver asked "[D]o the plays deal with the same facets of experience religion must also deal with?", and Beckett answered "Yes, for they deal with distress." (221) But obviously Beckett's aim is not that of going back to a Christian vision of the world, and his answer admits no doubt about that possibility. In fact in the same interview he claimed:

> Well, really there is [no religious significance in my plays] at all. I have no religious feeling. [...] My brother and mother got no value from their religion when they died. At the moment of crisis it had no more depth than an old school tie." (220)

This chapter does not aim to bring Beckett back to Christianity. Nevertheless, as shown, it is possible to draw some similarity between ideas and forces that permeate spiritual texts and Beckett's works. The "distress" mentioned by Beckett is only one of these forces. We will consider some others; confusion and weakness, the need to a fight in order to accomplish a duty, the need for a revolt against fixed structures, the lack of reliance in human qualities, the relationship between language and mystic experience and the insufficiency of rationality when dealing with mystic subjects. Notice that Beckett, discussing a picture by Schmidt-Rottluff in 1936

> found himself drawn into restating his own criterion of true art, in which he not only repeated his view that the authentic poem or picture was a prayer but developed

the image further than he had ever done up to that point: "the art (picture) that is a prayer sets up prayer, releases prayer in onlooker, i.e. *Priest*: Lord have mercy upon us. *People*: Christ have mercy upon us". (Knowlson, 237)

Beckett's view of art is extremely associated with religious feelings, although probably only at that time of his life.

The first sub-chapter, about the *Bhagavad-Gita*, tries to clarify and develop, with the help of spiritual texts, those concepts we have been confronted with in the chapter about Plato, and then it tries to show how widely these spiritual texts can be applied to Beckett's works; the second sub-chapter, about medieval mystics, is concerned with Beckett's possible use of a negative mysticism.

Bhagavad-Gita

In the *Bhagavad-Gita* we find an interesting passage. The choice of that Hindu text is due to the fact that a Christian text (especially the Bible) could lead to confusion because of Beckett's frequent allusions to Christian images. Beckett has once clearly stated that he had used those images because they were part of his culture, and for this reason only.[14] The choice of an Indian text should prevent every misunderstanding.[15]

Krishna, Arjuna's charioteer, draws up the chariot in the midst of the armies of both parties. Arjuna sees all the different grades of friends and relatives among his enemies and is "overwhelmed with compassion" (56). He does not want to fight and says to Krishna: "Now I am confused about my duty and have lost all composure because of miserly weakness. In this condition I am asking you to tell me for certain what is best for me." (81) Krishna answers.

Part I – "The Nothing to express"

> Considering your specific duty as a ksatriya [a person who gives protection from harm], you should know that there is no better engagement for you than fighting on religious principles; and so there is no need for hesitation. [...] If, however, you do not perform your religious duty of fighting, then you will certainly incur sins for neglecting your duties and thus lose your reputation as a fighter. (115-8)

In this short passage we can find many elements that have marked Beckett's composition process and that can be used to explain the terminology mentioned in the chapter about Plato. The first one is that of confusion and weakness. Arjuna confronted with the evidence of having to kill his cousins that he considers as brothers, his other relatives, his teachers and his friends, does not know what to do. Force of circumstances have obligated him to fight but he would rather not. Beckett is in a similar situation: he is forced to write although he does not know what about and how he should write. His battle is against the activity that haunts him most, i.e. the obligation to express. The relatives and friends that he has to kill, are his rational thoughts which he is fond of, but which prevent him from hearing the voice of the Muse. Arjuna's depressed state of mind is similar to Beckett's lack of power when the decision to write has to be taken. Arjuna and Beckett are so confused about their duty that they refuse it.

Krishna answers that for a warrior and a person who gives protection from harm there is no better engagement than fighting on religious principles. The first consideration that can be made is that Krishna does not obligate Arjuna to fight: he says that no better action can be performed but not that it is the only possibility. "There is no need for hesitation" he adds. Krishna claims that each person (or group of people) has his specific duties and has not to perform them hesitantly. Arjuna can thus accept or refuse to fight. He will have to bear the consequences of his decision: if he fights he performs his duty and, irrespective of success or defeat, he will be righteous; if he abstains from fighting he will be punished and lose his reputation as a fighter.[16] Arjuna can choose between action or refusal. Beckett has the same problem: he can decide if he wants to write or if he does not want to. Nobody and nothing obligate him. Like Arjuna, who decides not to fight, Beckett reaches the decision not to write, Arjuna because he has to kill all his relatives, Beckett because he has to admit the defeat of rationality. But they are not sure of what is righteous, Arjuna feels that his duty is to use his bow and arrows, and notwithstanding, sits on the chariot and refuses to fight; Beckett feels that he has to express but does not accept that fact. They honestly struggle with themselves: they do not give in to the rationally and emotionally best solution (I do not want to fight/write, therefore I do not fight/write), but dig into their conscience in order to find the right answer. What is interesting is that when they have decided to fight and to write, they do not take pleasure out of these actions. They carry them out because they know that these actions are the best solution to the situation they are confronted with, and because they are urged to do so (Arjuna by the person he considers an incarnation of God i.e. Krishna. Beckett by his necessity to express). This similarity between Arjuna (symbol of the righteous man who seeks knowledge and Truth) and Beckett shows how Beckett's research is deeply spiritual, and how seriously he engages in it.

Another interesting idea is that of the need of a fight. In order to accomplish his duty, Arjuna has to struggle. If he wants to be good and just, to be given back his kingdom, and to progress on the spiritual path, he has to defeat his enemies. Beckett has to do the same: he has to struggle against a way of expression which he considers useless or even harmful, he has to fight against a traditional view of poetry which concentrates on reproduction and not on real creativity, and he has to struggle against the difficulty of finding a revolutionary way of expression, which would enable him to express himself. His award would be that of having done what he is obligated to, to be at peace with himself and to reach a higher degree of consciousness of his inner life.

The hardest fight, for Arjuna and for Beckett, is that against themselves. Arjuna has to find his courage and noblesse again before he can battle; Beckett is constantly searching for himself, for his way of expression, for his concepts to become clear. Arjuna succeeds because he can rely on Krishna, his omniscient teacher, Beckett is condemned to an endless search because nobody helps him in his quest for Truth, and thus his results are never exhaustive.

The next element mentioned by Krishna in his speech is that of the divine origin of Arjuna's duty. He speaks of "religious duty" and of "sins for neglecting them". We have already seen that Krishna is not saying these words in order to force Arjuna to fight by frightening him with possible punishments. It is not a threat, it is the observation of a natural process: if he does not fight, something will happen and this result will be unpleasant because his action has not been performed according to his duties. Krishna speaks of sin because there is nothing worse than acting against one's own spiritual development. Arjuna's duty of fighting is described as religious because he has not chosen it but a divine force has ordered it. If Arjuna wants to progress spiritually, he has to obey that order.

This divine order has to be felt inside one's heart and one has to surrender to it (cf. Part III, Ch. 1. where I will concentrate on Moran's voice). Krishna calls this state "consciousness". "When your mind is no longer disturbed by the flowery language of the Vedas, and when it remains fixed in the trance of self-realisation, then you will have attained the divine consciousness" (141). We have already seen how Beckett in the dialogues with Georges Duthuit describes his disgust for that kind of art he considers mere representation of phenomena. He rejects it and spends great efforts to destroy it. Beckett is disturbed by what he considers the flowery language of the rational product of literature, he tries to remain fixed on himself to hear his inner voice, and his works contain an attempt to report his divine consciousness. Deirdre Bair, speaking of the writing period 1946-7, describes two indispensable elements which Beckett needs to comprehend that divine order, the necessity of silence and of solitude. "In the apartment, he was isolated and withdrawn, as if he were reliving what he had written, dredging so deep that he could not come back to the surface of his consciousness without painful effort." (377-8) Beckett writes at night and sleeps by day, he wants to be able to concentrate on himself, he wants to immerse himself in silence in order to become aware of that "divine consciousness" which originates and blossoms in his soul.[17] Beckett longs to comprehend that voice. Again Beckett approaches Arjuna and his prayers to Krishna in the middle of a battlefield. Both hear the voice of the Muse and the murmur of Truth inside their hearts, and have to silence their surroundings in order to comprehend it.

The last interesting aspect of the dialogue between Arjuna and Krishna is that of human defeat. Arjuna's reasonings are coherent and rational, his despair is real and justifiable, but Krishna gives them a relative importance. Krishna affirms that consciousness stems from the giving up of those reasonings of the mind. "One who is not disturbed in mind even amidst the threefold miseries or elated when there is happiness, and who is free from attachment, fear and anger, is called a sage of steady mind." (144) Krishna does not consider Arjuna's feelings important because they are troubling his mind which should concentrate on "divine consciousness" only. Arjuna, in fact, gives up his cares and relies on Krishna, symbol of that consciousness (cf. the already quoted passage "Now I am confused about my duty and have lost all composure because of miserly weakness. In this condition I am asking you to tell me for certain what is best for me.", 81). It is the surrender of human nature to divine awareness, it is the will to subjugate the confusion of the mind to the harmony of detachment from emotional reactions.

Beckett is obsessed by this dichotomy and his works often deal with that shift of emphasis from man towards divinity. His "there is nothing to express, together with the obligation to express" can be meant as the opposition of the vacuity of the mind (human) to the necessity of awareness (divine). Beckett feels that consciousness as an obligation in that his mind strongly refuses to be silent and prefers to wander endlessly from subject to subject, without any coherence or purpose, making it difficult to hear the other voice. In *The Unnamable* Beckett writes: "That's to lull me, till I imagine I hear myself saying, myself at last, to myself at last, that it can't be they, speaking thus, that it can only be I, speaking thus. Ah if I could only find a voice of my own, in all this babble." (320) The unnamable longs for "a voice of his own" (divine consciousness), but he cannot find it because "this babble" (created by his mind) prevents him. The apparent contradiction in Beckett is that he mixes up these two ways of expression. When he writes at the end of *The Unnamable* "I can't go on, I'll go on", he means that he cannot go on saying nonsense because he longs for consciousness, but he is obliged to continue by his ignorance of where and how to describe it. Beckett wants to express his consciousness but he is only able to express random thoughts that occasionally hint at it. It is here that Beckett partially fails, if confronted with Arjuna. Beckett never accepts his consciousness because everything is filtered through his mind. Or, in other words, Beckett never admits the defeat of the human part of man in favour of his divine one. Beckett does not subjugate his thoughts to the voice of the Muse.

How is this possible? What has brought Beckett to refuse his inadequate mind but not to accept divine consciousness? To what extent is he refusing that consciousness? How much is he ignoring it? And how much does he need it and is attracted by it? One way to answer these questions is to analyse other people's behaviour in similar situations. I have decided to concentrate on medieval mystics because that religious and literary movement presents some analogies with Beckett's composition process.[18]

Even Emile Michel Cioran could "very easily imagine Beckett, a few centuries back, in a bare cell unsullied by any decoration, not even a crucifix." (338)

Medieval Mystics: Meister Eckhart and "De Imitatione Christi"

Louis Cognet in his *Introduction aux mystiques rhéno-flamands*, affirms that mysticism became widespread when the official and outward appearance of the Catholic Church disappointed many of its best souls.

> [B]eaucoup d'âmes, parmi les meilleurs, déçues par les formes extérieures et officielles du christianisme, se rejettent vers une ardente vie intérieure de type souvent mystique, et cherchent à promouvoir de l'intérieur une réforme du catholicisme en diffusant autour d'elles une spiritualité de ce genre. (20)

These people dedicated themselves to their inner life in order to reform the church from inside by means of their example as mystics. This mechanism is similar to Beckett's revolution of form and contents, because Beckett has conducted it from the inside. To criticise the forms and the contents of literature and to introduce new ones, he has composed novels, plays, poems.

Mystics wanted to communicate their experience of God thanks to their works; Beckett, with the aid of his works, wants to show his disgust at how feelings and situations have been, and are, represented. It is his way of rejecting those structures that he finds completely corrupted by long (and improper) use.

But Beckett revolts against the structures in which he has to fit as a writer. His refusal to use them is the key to new forms of expression; he wants to show that new forms can be found in spite of the corruption of the old ones. Beckett's reaction is a consequence of the decay of content in favour of form. He wants to create something new, as stated in the first of the *Three Dialogues*: "Yet I speak of an art turning from it [the feasible] in disgust, weary of its puny exploits, weary of pretending to be able, of being able, of doing a little better the same old thing, of going a little further along a dreary road." (139) Beckett, as already seen, is not looking for a variation in the expression of a subject, he is looking for a new way of expressing a completely new subject. The abuse of forms and of their authority, caused by a general weakening of inventiveness, separates them from their contents. Beckett's reaction is a revaluation of a quest which puts no reliance on human qualities. Again we are presented with Beckett's mind-soul dichotomy. On the one hand, we have Beckett's rational decision to destroy literature and expression as they are generally intended, on the other hand we have that (for Beckett) still unknown new way of expression. Unfortunately, he tries to develop it by means of his thoughts (cf. the section about Meister Eckhart).

Beckett puts no reliance on human qualities because he feels that they do not reach the whole of Truth but nevertheless is not able to abandon them in favour of the voice of the Muse, of spirituality. Silvano Simoni, in his introduction to the *Imitatio Christi*, writes:

> le verità metafisiche sono al di fuori della certezza razionale [...] se si vorrà conoscere Dio non resterà da seguire se non la via dell'amore, lo slancio interiore del cuore, l'unica altra forma di conoscenza che resta, e cioè quella dell'intuizione. (11)

Simoni claims that, rational reason being insufficient, the only way for the comprehension of metaphysical truths is intuition. And Saint Augustine affirms:

> Et inde admonitus redire ad memet ipsum intravi in

intima mea duce te et potui, quoniam <u>factus es adiutor meus</u>.[19] Intravi et vidi qualicumque oculo animae meae, supra mentem meam lucem inconmutabilem. (*Confessionum*, VII, 10)

Augustine enters into the intimacy of his heart and with the eyes of his soul, guided by God himself, he sees above his intelligence, above his soul, an immutable light. It is thus not through intelligence, and not thanks to one's soul either, that the *unknown* can be grasped.

The term 'intuition' fits very well for Beckett because he is looking for something (consciousness) which is out of rational reach. But Beckett is strongly interested in rationality, also if he is interested in its annihilation. His works always contain characters with an agonising rationality. Beckett does not thoroughly refuse the products of the mind, but he sees its limits and is disappointed by them. He would like to explain his intuition by means of rationality, but fails: his accusations are not sterile but full of an anger produced by disappointment. Intuition must thus stem from something different and we have already decided to call that origin divine consciousness. Beckett is unable to present a rationalisation of his intuition and the best he can produce are images that hint at it. His works are a mixture of delusion for the insufficiency of rationality and of interest for his involvement in his intuition.[20]

How are his delusion and his interest expressed in his work? And how are they mixed? Rudolf Arnheim, in an essay on disorder and order, helps us to answer these questions by giving a definition of entropy: "entropy is defined as the quantitative measure of the degree of disorder in a system." (8) Systems, he claims, are of two contradictory kinds: on the one hand we have those which follow the Second Law of Thermodynamics, which states "that the entropy of the world strives towards a maximum" (9) i.e. in the material universe disorder increases. On the other hand, we have the fact that human beings basically strive towards order in what they create. To reconcile this discrepancy, Arnheim points out that the law of entropy reflects not only the disintegration of material form, but also a general tendency to enhance equilibrium by tension reduction.

> Modern science, then, maintains on the one hand that nature, both organic and inorganic, strives towards a state of order and that man's actions are governed by the same tendency. It maintains on the other hand that physical systems move towards a state of maximum disorder. (8)

Nature and human actions, Arnheim writes, tend towards order; while physical events tend to the maximal degree of disorder. But even visual arts suggest the same movement.

> Today we no longer regard the universe as the cause of our own undeserved troubles but perhaps, on the contrary, as the last refuge from the mismanagement of our earthly affairs. Even so, the law of entropy continues to make for a bothersome discrepancy in the humanities and helps to maintain the artificial separation from the natural sciences. Lancelot L. Whyte, acutely aware of the problem, formulated it by asking: "What is the relation of the two cosmic tendencies: towards mechanical disorder (entropy principle) and towards geometrical order (in crystals, molecules, organisms, etc.)?"
>
> The visual arts have recently presented us with two stylistic trends which, at first look, may seem quite different from each other but which the present investigation may reveal to have common roots. On the one hand, there is a display of extreme simplicity [...] The other tendency, relying on accidental or deliberately produced disorder. [...] Surely the popular use of the

notion of entropy has changed. If during the last century it served to diagnose, explain, and deplore the degradation of culture, it now produces a positive rationale for "minimal" art and the pleasures of chaos. (10-11)

Beckett's struggle is similar to what Arnheim describes to be the two stylistic trends in visual arts. On the one hand Beckett tries to reach an ordered perfection (of which he only has an intuition), on the other he is hindered by the disorder implicit in chaos and which stems from trying to rationalise it. In fact, rationality tries to draw a conclusion from an amount of data which is not large enough to allow a rationalisation of the intuition, and consequently rationality acts mechanically, without being able to complete, humanise and order the results it obtains. It is interesting to analyse how and why rationality acts in this manner. How is it possible to affirm that it is working on an insufficient amount of data? What does *rationality acts mechanically* mean? And how does this process take place? Hugo Friedrich writes that

> [d]ie Wirklichkeit ist aus der räumlichen, zeitlichen, sachlichen und seelischen Ordnung herausgelöst und den Unterscheidungen entzogen, wie sie einer normalen Weltorientierung notwendig sind: zwischen schön und häßlich, zwischen Nähe und Ferne, zwischen Licht und Schatten, zwischen Schmerz und Freude, zwischen Erde und Himmel. (11)

Truth is not completely contained in the structures which compose a purely rational analysis, nor is it subject to comparative processes. Truth has an additional part which rationality tries to reach by applying the apophatic method, i.e. by negating all the peculiarities which are not part of its limited nature. Beckett constantly applies the apophatic method but he rejects its conclusions. As we have already seen, his language is not exhaustive; he is always negating man's peculiarities (cf. *Endgame, Waiting for Godot*), he longs for silence but yet continues to search in the realm of rationality (cf. the trilogy).[21]

At a certain point, this method reaches an impasse, when everything has been negated but the essence of Truth has still not been understood. At this point the "absolute distinction and tension between the language of utterance [rationality] and the immutability of God [truth]" (Wolosky, 179) has to be assumed and the power of rationality is defeated. But rationality reacts to this frustration, emphasising its action. Wolosky describes its reaction as the reduction of "space and any activity within it to pure extension - to purely geometrical and mathematical elements." (169) Rationality tries to exclude everything that "resists quantitative expression; passion, hope, grief, pleasure. Only number, figure, magnitude, and duration remain." (169-70) The unnamable's indifference towards any showing of feelings, and his need to continually rephrase and repeat the causes of his monologue are a clear example of this mechanism.

Beckett's rationality fails to apply St. Augustine's distinction between "numbers as they are used in counting things" and the "principle of number by which we count." (quoted in Wolosky, 172) Beckett's use of mathematics tries to destroy the intuition he has had at another level; his geometrical structures are a "recuperation of unpredictable negativity" (Budick and Iser, xviii), because they reject Beckett's divine consciousness, condemning him to an endless search. An example is *Quad* with its strongly defined geometrical structure with no other meaning than itself and the way it is performed.

Meister Eckhart is a theorist of mysticism; he often describes God's peculiarities, the mechanisms of the relationship man-God, the paths to follow in order to establish that relationship, etc. His ontology is based on a theory of being that creates the bases of a mystic relationship. A mystic experience has to be elaborated and justified by means of dialectics in order to let it become a deduction.[22] God, Meister Eckhart claims, is absolute transcendence, and if one compares humans to divinity, one has to admit that human beings are a miserable product. In order to become aware of one's soul, it is necessary to negate one's human peculiarities. It is the only way to contact the divine. Bliss and real knowledge are thus not rational. Only by going back to God, can humans reveal their true reality. But to be able to go back to God, it is necessary that the soul has abandoned all relationship with earthly corruption.

The unnamable seems to have abandoned the world, and he constantly claims that his living "here" makes it impossible for him to have any contact whatsoever with "there", but his mind is not detached from the world of the living. "They" (his rational part) prevent him from going silent and from leaving definitively "there". In Part III we will see how Beckett nears himself to Eckhart. Beckett's characters often speak of their attempt to apply these mechanisms. Beckett's characters cannot mention their spirituality, but their search is similar to Eckhart's, and applies the same elements (e.g. silence, negations, contradictions).

Eckhart, in some of his German sermons, describes the concept of *Gotheit*, i.e. the absolute being, the divine essence independent of whatever relationship, and different from what he calls *Got*.[23] According to Eckhart, it is thus impossible to talk about that *Gotheit*, because knowledge and language create a relationship which is thoroughly and completely negated by the same concept of the divine. It is here that Eckhart encounters a fundamental problem, namely that it is not possible to speak of divinity because in that particular situation knowledge and language create a relationship which is radically denied. Eckhart resolves that contradiction by claiming that *Gotheit*, does not exist for human beings, in that they can neither talk about it, nor can they speculate about that concept. Eckhart applies here Augustine's *regio dissimilitudinis*, i.e. the distance that separates human beings from the *Gotheit*.

> Et cum te primum cognovi, tu assumisti me, ut viderem esse, quod viderem, et mondum me esse, qui viderem. Et reverberasti infirmitatem aspectus mei radians in me vehementer, et contremui amore et horrore: et inveni longe me esse a te in regione dissimilitudinis, tamquam audirem vocem tuam de excelso. (*Confessionum*, VII, 10)

Augustine describes here the ascent of the soul towards the divine, and he claims that he was not able to see what God wanted him to look at. Augustine finds himself far away from God and himself, and he hears His voice coming from above. God becomes thus unnameable because of his immensity, and his real name is unnameable too, it becomes an unsayable/unknowable concept. The human soul, through human intelligence, can never be satisfied because it longs for a name and a definition of what it calls God (and which is something else, that escapes its partial definitions) and this fact produces an insatiable frustration. Meister Eckhart concludes that when faced with divinity, only silence is proper. A speech on the matter of divinity is only possible if the apophatic method is applied, i.e. all peculiarities of the limited being are negated.

Beckett is constantly concerned with these topics and, as already seen, constantly applies the apophatic method but he refuses its conclusions. The unnamable seems to reside in Saint Augustine's *regio dissimilitudinis*, where the distance between human beings and Eckhart's *Gotheit* becomes infinite, where human intelligence tries to elaborate concepts too wide to be grasped by rationality. The unnamable tries to name what could give him definitive peace, but he tries to do it with "their" words. Silence seems to be out reach; it is the unnamable's definitive defeat.

Mysticism

The last part of this chapter deals with some concepts taken from Thomas A Kempis's *De imitatione Christi*. Beckett was well acquainted with the *Imitation of Christ*. In a letter to Thomas MacGreevy written on 10 March 1935, he quotes the A Kempis text both in Latin and English and "comments astutely on it" (Knowlson, 179).

The aim of the discussion of thoughts taken from that work is that of, once more, showing their similarity with ideas and statements that can be found in Beckett's works. I have decided to compare Molloy, Moran, Malone and the unnamable to some extracts taken from the *Imitatione Christi*.[24] Molloy with his rambling through Ballybaba is the only character in the trilogy to have contact with the physical world, although his perceptions are already distorted by his dwelling in his mother's room and by his confused memory. In the first Book of the *Imitatione Christi*, which lists useful warnings for the leading of a spiritual life, Thomas A Kempis claims:

> So long as we live in this world we cannot be without tribulation and temptation. [...] There is no man that is altogether free from temptations whilst he liveth on earth [...] Many seek to fly temptations, and fall more grievously into them. By flight alone we cannot overcome, but by patience and true humility we become stronger than all our enemies. (I, xiii, 1-3)

Molloy is constantly confronted with "tribulation and temptation". His whole rambling with the innumerable mishaps and forgettings that prevent him from visiting his mother are a clear example. To visit his mother is the only task Molloy tries to accomplish (when he remembers it), and thus what diverts him, has to be considered a temptation. "And though there were many things I could do without thinking, not knowing what I was going to do until it was done, and not even then, going to my mother was not one of them."

Part I – "The Nothing to express"

(*Molloy*, 29) Molloy's tribulation is caused by his mental confusion which makes him forget where his mother lives, where he is, and even that he is looking for his mother's home.

"[A]ny man [...] consider[s] and thoroughly weigh his state of banishment, and the many perils wherewith his soul is environed." (I, xxi, 1) Molloy's temptations and perils are caused by his mind, too. "My feet, you see, never took me to my mother unless they received a definite order to do so." (*Molloy*, 29) And Molloy often forgets to give that order or, if he remembers, he soon forgets what he was looking for and why. Molloy provides himself with both tribulations and temptations, there is no evil presence that tempts him. Nevertheless the result is the same. Molloy avoids doing his duty, and this causes his frustration and ends in his definitive defeat when he learns that his mother is dead. "Many seek to fly temptations, and fall more grievously into them." (I, xiii, 3) Thomas A Kempis suggests the solution to these temptations, and it is here that Beckett detaches himself most from the Author of the *Imitatio*. "By flight alone we cannot overcome, but by patience and true humility we become stronger than all our enemies". (I, xiii, 3) Beckett, instead, shows that there is no possible accomplishment of our duties. Molloy waits too much, until his mother dies, and at this moment, he is motionless and starts to forget how to express himself. Patience and humility (and on this occasion we could interpret Molloy's crawling, at the end of *Molloy*, as a sort of parody of religious prostrating) are no solution for Molloy, on the contrary they cause Molloy's defeat.

Molloy often seems to follow Thomas A Kempis's suggestion that "thou canst not possess perfect liberty unless thou wholly renounce thyself." (III, xxxii, 1) Molloy is renouncing himself, he clearly states it at the beginning of the novel. "[N]ow it's nearly the end. [...] All grows dim. A little more and you'll go blind. It's in the head. It doesn't work any more, it says, I don't work any more." (*Molloy*, 9-10) Molloy hopes to reach an end, the "nothing more"

(10), which should lead him to "perfect liberty". Again, what is lacking in Beckett is a hereafter, a place different and apart from life.

Going on to Moran, the following extract could be applied to the changes he undergoes during his journey to Ballybaba.

> My son, trust not to thy feelings, for whatever they be now, they will quickly be changed towards some other thing. As long as thou livest, thou art subject to change, even against thy will; so that thou art at one time merry, at another sad; at one time quiet, at another troubled; now devout, now undevout; now diligent; now listless; now grave, and now light. But he that is wise and well instructed in the Spirit standeth fast upon these changing things; not heeding what he feeleth in himself, or which way the wind of instability bloweth; but that the whole intent of his mind may be to the right and the best end. (III, xxxiii, 1)

Moran's account of his mission to "see about Molloy" (*Molloy*, 85), perfectly fits Thomas A Kempis's description. At the beginning of his journey he feels secure, but then, the nearer he gets to Molloy, the more he changes, losing his rationality and his ability to move. Molloy is, for Moran, the "wind of instability" described by Thomas; Molloy destroys Moran, he is a sort of "selva oscura" like the one in which Dante lost himself at the beginning of the *Comedy*. Moran is not able to maintain his mind "to the right and the best end," and this causes his defeat. Beckett diverts from the *Imitatio* in that he gives to one of his characters (Molloy) the possibility of destroying Moran even without meeting him; he creates a sort of omnicomprehensive negative divinity. Thomas A Kempis continues:

> But he that is wise and well instructed in the Spirit standeth fast upon these changing things; not heeding

what he feeleth in himself, or which way the wind of instability bloweth; but that the whole intent of his mind may be to the right and the best end. (III, xxxiii, 1)

In the second part of his account, Moran speaks about a voice he hears. "I have spoken of a voice giving me orders, or rather advice. It was on the way home I heard it for the first time." (156) The reader could think that Beckett is introducing a positive force in Moran's life, that will transform the secret agent into "he that is wise and well instructed in the Spirit". But Moran's "I paid no attention to it." (156), shows, once again, how Beckett, after deceiving us, goes on in his personal and rebellious way. Moran hears the voice but does not obey its orders.

Going on to the second novel of the trilogy, we encounter Malone with his stories and inventories. Malone has lost his memory. "As to the events that led up to my fainting and to which I can hardly have been oblivious, at the time, they have left no discernible trace, on my mind" (168), which is considered to be a positive fact by the Author of the *Imitatione Christi*.

> Cease from an inordinate desire of knowledge, for therein is much distraction and deceit. [...] The more thou knowest, and the better thou understandest, the more strictly shalt thou be judged, unless thy life be also the more holy. (I, ii, 2-3)

Malone's desire to be dead as soon as possible is also considered positive by Thomas A Kempis.

> Why dost thou here gaze about, since this is not the place of thy rest? In heaven ought to be thy home, and

all earthly things are to be looked upon as it were by the way. (II, i, 4)

We have seen that Molloy was looking for his mother and this caused his rambling and his mental confusion; Malone, on the contrary, has lost all his past and is unable to describe his present. "It is the present I must establish" (169). Malone could thus seem the perfect spiritual seeker, but this changes as soon as he starts to tell his stories and digresses from his purposes.

Thomas A Kempis affirms that it is not possible to be in peace when the content of our conversations is not appropriate.

> What will become of us in the end, who begin so early to wax lukewarm? Woe be unto us, if we will so give ourselves unto ease as if all were now peace and safety, when as yet there appeareth no sign of true holiness in our conversation! (I, xxii, 7) Very quickly there will be an end of thee here; see therefore to thy state: to-day man is; tomorrow he is gone. (*De Imitatione Christi*, I, xxiii, 1)

Malone thinks he will soon be dead, but his words are "a play" (166). And Kempis's menace to be careful about what we are saying because life can suddenly end, does not apply to Malone, who is waiting for death. Beckett thus destroys the tension Thomas has set by means of his warnings, and Malone's longing for death turns the idea that speeches have to be appropriate upside down. What could be defined "appropriate" if you are gratefully waiting to die? Thomas's answer is "Let thy thoughts be on the Highest, and thy prayers for mercy directed unto Christ, without ceasing." (II, i, 4) Malone seems to live in "peace and safety" in that he has no contact with the world anymore, but in fact he is not detached from it, and his stories bring him back there to where "true holiness" (I, xxii, 7) is not present.

Malone's words have not the aim of helping him to be released from grief, they are only sounds that fill the silence he is afraid of.

Why is Malone speaking? He says that "[w]hile waiting I shall tell myself stories" (165), but let us consider what the author of the *Imitatione Christi* affirms about thoughts and words.

> O what do I inwardly suffer, whilst in my mind I dwell on things heavenly, and presently in my prayers a multitude of carnal fancies rise up to me! [...] For oftentimes I am not there, where I stand or sit, but rather I am there, whither my thoughts do carry me. Where my thoughts are, there am I; and commonly there are my thoughts, where my affection is. (III, xlviii, 5)

Malone gives space to his rambling mind that starts telling stories, and this diverts him from his detachment from the world. He speaks in order to get back, by means of rationality, to the world he says he would like to leave. His mind follows his casual stories and thus fails to apply Thomas A Kempis's "dwelling on things heavenly." What is frustrating is that Malone would like to apply those rules but then refuses to do it, or in Kempis's words "because the whole man doth slide off into outward things; and unless he speedily repent, he settleth down in them, and that willingly." (III, xliv, 2) Malone finds his stories boring, but he is not able -and does not want- to stop telling them. This causes his defeat.

Thomas A Kempis describes, at the beginning of his *Imitatione*, the way to lead a spiritual life. One of his hints is to avoid useless speeches.

> Fly the tumult of the world as much as thou canst; for the treating of worldly affairs is a great hindrance, although it be done with sincere intention; For we are

quickly defiled and enthralled by vanity. Oftentimes I could wish that I had held my peace when I have spoken; and that I had not been in company. Why do we so willingly speak and talk one with another, when notwithstanding we seldom cease our converse before we have hurt our conscience? The cause why we so willingly talk, is for that by discoursing one with another, we seek to receive comfort one of another, and desire to ease our mind wearied with many thoughts: And we very willingly talk and think of those things which we most love or desire; or of those things which we feel to be against us. But alas, oftentimes in vain, and to no end; for this outward comfort is the cause of no small loss of inward and divine consolation. (I, x, 1-2)

The unnamable strives for silence, but he is not able to become silent. And his speech is the hindrance to his being satisfied. Why is the unnamable speaking? As we have already seen, Meister Eckhart helps us to suggest that the unnamable speaks because his mind is not detached from "there". Thomas A Kempis suggests that when we talk it is to receive comfort and to ease our wearied mind; the unnamable claims that he is forced to speak by some people he calls "they", and he cannot escape from their exhortations to talk. "Unless a man be set free from all creatures, he cannot wholly attend unto divine things. And therefore are there so few contemplative, for that few can wholly withdraw themselves from things created and perishing." (III, xxxi, 1) The unnamable is a potential contemplative character in that he would like to be silent and to withdraw himself from whatever influence from "there", but he fails because "they" do not leave him alone and force him to speak. Thus the unnamable speaks, but not about things he loves or about what he feels against himself; he just allows words to exit his mouth. In fact he receives no consolation, as Kempis suggests.

To conclude, Thomas A Kempis claims: "My son, I ought to be thy supreme and ultimate end, if thou desire to be truly blessed." (III, ix, 1) The four characters of the trilogy seem to be looking for the same thing the Author of the *Imitatione* is searching for; a less precarious relationship, truth, detachment from life, silence, the ultimate end. But they all fail.[25]

Summary

We have seen that Beckett's works are composed following mechanisms which are similar to those described in, or deducible from, texts concerned with religion. With the aid of the *Bhagavad-Gita* we have observed that Samuel Beckett's life presents aspects which can be found in the description of a righteous man; he is urged by a voice that pushes him to a restless quest for what we have called divine consciousness. This consciousness does not originate from man's rational part, but from his spiritual part, and it is the force that every spiritual searcher longs for. We have also seen that a fight, inside the searcher's heart, is needed in order to understand what is spiritual and what is part of a rational fear. We have then considered Beckett's attitude towards that consciousness.

We have concluded, with the help of Meister Eckhart and of Thomas A Kempis, that Beckett's straight interest is for rationality but his mind is unable to explain his spiritual part. Beckett's reaction is of rage at the limits of rationality, and of a refusal to accept that rationally unexplainable part. We have then seen how this rejection is not enough to extinguish the force of his intuition and we have noticed how these aspects have influenced Beckett's compositional process both in its contents and in its lack of form, conferring on them a universality of unexpressed concepts.

I would like to conclude this chapter with Simoni's words (my translation).

> The *Imitatio Christi* engenders, nearly without our noticing it, that comfort, that serenity, that peace, that joy, which we are always looking for and which not always our lives reserve for us. This happens because the *Imitatio* reveals, to ourselves, our soul with our passions and our weaknesses, with our deficiencies and our limits, with our uncertainties and our indecision, with our wishes and our hopes, our joys and our pains, with our enthusiasms and our depressions, and showing that we, like Dante writes in *Inferno* xxvi, 119-20: "fatti non foste a viver come bruti, ma per seguire virtude e conoscenza." (16)

With all the corrections and limitations we have considered, Beckett's *unknown* achieves the same result.

PART II – "THE NOTHING WITH WHICH TO EXPRESS AND THE NOTHING FROM WHICH TO EXPRESS"

DIRECT PHILOSOPHICAL INFLUENCES ON BECKETT

INTRODUCTION

The *unknown* haunts Samuel Beckett and obliges him to write. In Part I, I have tried to give a definition of this force that spurs Beckett to create. In Part II, I will concentrate on Beckett's writing process, on the levels on which the *unknown* produces a result, that is the "nothing with which to express" and the "nothing from which to express". How does the Irish writer compose his works? Which are (some of) the literary sources that have helped him to develop his way of expressing the *unknown*? Beckett's awareness of the hindrance he feels towards writing implies that he must have applied some kind of theory to his writing process. But Beckett has not spoken nor written (unless it be sparingly and on particular works only) about how he composed his novels and plays, and so we must try to reconstruct that process. There are two ways of proceeding to achieve this result, to rebuild the theory from its results (i.e. the works themselves, and this will be done in Part III), or to deduce it from other writers' poetic theories which Beckett knew and which could have helped him to form his own.

I have considered two authors' direct philosophical influences on Beckett. The first author is Dante Alighieri. I have analysed Dante's literary theories and his cosmology, which have been condensed and elaborated by Beckett. The aim of this comparison is that of showing how both Dante's and Beckett's poetry are an attempt to create a new way of expression (and, consequently, a new reality), Dante by creating a new language (the Italian ideolect), while Beckett, by destroying grammatical, syntactic, lexical rules and meaning, creates a sort of non-language (or rather, a way of expression which is to a certain extent not subject to conventional rules). Making reference to Dante's *Epistola XIII* to Cangrande della Scala, I have analysed those elements that, according to Dante, have to be considered before reading a doctrinal work, and I have applied them to Beckett's work. I have shown how Beckett's works produce a result on several levels at the same time (literal, allegorical, moral, anagogic). I have then considered the two levels that can be found in Beckett's work, the literal one, which copes with the destruction of traditional rules, and the allegorical one, which hints at the spiritual part. To enrich this view, I have added the comparison Beckett - Petrarch, showing how they both see that language cannot fully describe what they need to say. I have then considered the episode of Belacqua (*Purgatorio*, iv) and that of the Ante-Inferno (*Inferno*, iii).

The second chapter of Part II is devoted to Giambattista Vico. A first introductory part concentrates on the polemics between Vico and Descartes. On the one hand Descartes claims that history cannot be considered a subject for the scientific world, on the other Vico affirms that it is possible to make a science out of it. History is a human product, and thus, scientifically, shows the evolution of human beings and of societies. Many important Vichian topics are present in Beckett's works e.g. the limits of human beings to comprehend Nature, expressed in the "verum-factum" theory, or the fact that the historic and social worlds have been created by humans. Even Vico's theoretical scheme has been reconsidered by the Irish poet. Vico wanted to bring together Plato (theoretician of the existence of a universal knowledge which operates in humans, spur to Beckett's obligation to express), and Tacitus (who is not concerned with ideal human beings, but considers them as they are, cf. Beckett's characters) by means of philology in order to create what Vico, quoting Bacon, calls "l'universal repubblica delle lettere" (notice the similarity with the monologues spoken by Molloy and Moran in *Molloy*). Less obvious but even more interesting are the influences of ideas like that of the presence in humans of fundamental aspects (theorised by Plato) and developed by Vico with the name of "idea eterna"; the subdivision of history into three ages, theocratic, heroic and civilised; the consideration of language, poetry and myth as instruments of extreme importance in the development of human beings and societies; the existence of an ideal project towards which human beings tend with their behaviour. These themes have often been revised in a negative way by Beckett, especially in the trilogy *Molloy, Malone Dies, The Unnamable*.

DANTE ALIGHIERI

This chapter is concerned with Dante Alighieri's view of poetry and poetic forms. Dante is useful because he has explained his own work and he has built a rather complex theory of writing. Dante accompanies his artistic works with a continuous reflection on his own life in order to join the reasons for his living and writing on an ideological level and in order to set up his way of writing on strict and exact norms with the purpose of getting a total correspondence between contents and style. The comparison between Beckett and Dante is not to be understood as a comparison of two existing theories, but as a mixture of the two ways of proceeding mentioned above. Dante's theory, applied to Beckett's works, should help us to comprehend Beckett's poetic expression.

Beckett first read Dante in 1925, taking Thomas Rudmose-Brown's course in Dante's *Divine Comedy* at Trinity College, Dublin, and working with Bianca Esposito, a private tutor in Dublin, with whom he analysed the *Comedy* and the *Vita Nuova* (Knowlson, 52). He was fascinated by the poetry of the Florentine. References and allusions to Dante often appear in Beckett. Belacqua, the main character of *More Pricks Than Kicks*, is named after a character appearing in Purgatory (iv, 98-135); Malacoda is the title of a poem and the name of a devil in Hell (xxi-xxii); Beckett's essay on Joyce is based in part on the Italian poet. The trilogy is filled with reference to the Florentine: Molloy and Malone speak about Sordello (*Molloy*, 12; *Malone Dies*, 262); Malone speaks of the "fires and ice of hell" (166) and of "how is it the moon where Cain toils bowed beneath his burden never sheds its light on my face" (203) like Dante in *Inf.* xx, 124-7; the unnamable wonders: "Are there other pits, deeper down? To which one accedes by mine?" (268), and he speaks about Dante's description of Ulisses's last voyage (*Inf.*, xxvi, 85-142).

The galley-man, bound for the Pillars of Hercules, who drops his sweep under cover of night and crawls between the thwarts, towards the rising sun, unseen by the guard, praying for storm. Except that I've stopped praying for anything. No, no, I'm still a supplicant. I'll get over it, between now and the last voyage, on this leaden sea. It's like the other madness, the mad wish to know, to remember, one's transgressions. (309)

Like Dante, Beckett speaks about a "last voyage" beyond the Pillars of Hercules; Ulisses will die with his crew when he nears the mountain of Purgatory, because, Dante suggests, human rationality and the need to understand will be frustrated by God's mystery. The unnamable with his babbling and inability to be silent demonstrates a similar theory.

Shortly before dying, early in 1989, when Beckett was moved to a nursing home, his schoolboy copy of Dante's *Divine Comedy* was one of his favourite possessions (Gussow, 3). It is thus probable that also the best known works by Beckett, although lacking literal references to Dante, contain theoretical items taken from the Florentine.

Dante's Epistola to Cangrande della Scala

Dante's *Epistola XIII* was sent to Cangrande della Scala in 1317. In it Dante dedicates his *Paradiso* to Cangrande and, most important, he gives us an "accessus ad auctorem" i.e. a general introduction to the reading of his work, especially of his *Comedy*. This epistle contains first an explicative comment on the literal meaning of the *Comedy*, and then comments on its allegorical meaning, in order to make clear the conceptual framework and development of the philosophical and religious truth of the text.

Part II – "The Nothing with which to express and the Nothing from which to express"

The *Epistola* starts with a general introduction which presents some general aspects of the *Commedia*. Dante presents those elements that have to be considered before reading a doctrinal work. "Sex igitur sunt que in principio cuiusque doctrinalis operis inquirenda sunt, videlicet subiectum, agens, forma, finis, libri titulus, et genus phylosophie." (608) To have access to all the levels of meaning of a work, six elements are essential: the first one, "subjectum" or "operis intentio" is about the work's material; the second, "agens" or "causa efficiens", is the character who performs the action; the third, "forma" or "causa formalis" is about the structure of the work and of its contents; the fourth, "finis" or "utilitas" deals with the aim of the work, its "causa finalis"; the fifth, "libri titulus" or "inscription" is the title; and the sixth "genus phylosophie" tries to define to which philosophical principles the work refers.

Dante starts by discussing the subject ("subiectum"). In his Comedy, the subject is defined as multiple.

> [N]am primus sensus est qui habetur per litteram, alius est qui habetur per significata per litteram. Et primus dicitur litteralis, secundus vero allegoricus sive moralis sive anagogicus. Qui modus tractandi, ut melius pateat, potest considerari in hiis versibus: "In exitu Israel de Egipto, domus Iacob de populo barbaro, facta est Iudea sanctificatio eius, Israel potestas eius." Nam si ad litteram solam inspiciamus, significatur nobis exitus filiorum Israel de Egipto, tempore Moysis; si ad allegoriam, nobis significatur nostra redemptio facta per Christum; si ad moralem sensum, significatur nobis conversio anime de luctu et miseria peccati ad statum gratie; si ad anagogicum, significatur exitus anime sancte ab huius corruptionis servitute ad eterne glorie libertatem. (610)

The first meaning is the one we perceive from the words

of the text; the other one is what we want the words of the text to mean. The first meaning is called literal meaning, the second is called allegorical or moral or anagogic. To better explain these ways of considering this matter we can take the following verses: "When Israel went out from Egypt, the house of Jacob from a people of strange language, Judah became God's sanctuary, Israel his dominion". If we consider the words, the text means that the sons of Israel left Egypt at the time of Moses, if we consider the allegory, it means that we are saved by the birth of Christ; if we consider the moral meaning, it means the passage of the soul from the darkness and sadness of sin to a state of grace; if we consider the anagogic meaning, it means the passage of the blessed soul from the slavery of earthly corruption to the freedom of eternal glory. (my translation)

Dante divides literal meaning from the allegorical, the moral and the anagogic one. The literal meaning is, in the quoted example, that the Hebrews left Egypt when Moses lived. In the trilogy, there are apparently several literal meanings: we have a tramp's and a detective's journey through a region called Ballybaba, a series of stories narrated by a dying man, and, finally, we are presented with a bodiless man soliloquising on the reasons for his monologue. But, in fact, the result of a literal reading would bring the reader to the conclusion that Beckett writes nonsense. There is no cohesion, no certainty and even no real facts, because the filters Molloy, Moran, Malone and the unnamable consciously apply to the facts and thoughts they describe make it extremely difficult to accept them as true. Beckett destroys the literal sense of the trilogy in that "per litteram" there is not only one fixed meaning, but several, and all of these are continuously negated and contradicted. What Dante considers the first and most easily comprehensible meaning of a written work, is transformed by

Part II – "The Nothing with which to express and the Nothing from which to express"

Beckett in self negation. The plot is a non-plot, the foundation on which the other meanings should rest is non-existent. Readers are forced to look somewhere else for meaning, it is not possible to read the trilogy as an explicit text because the conclusion one would draw is that there is no meaning. This could be a conclusion, but readers are spurred on to look for a sense in what they have read by neglecting the literal sense, because they feel that there is something more than mere nonsense. This lack of literal meaning is one of the reasons why Beckett's prose has been neglected by people who love him through his plays. In *Godot*, Didi's and Gogo's act of waiting is something real, it makes sense, and is easily perceived by the audience. Of course the audience may be upset by the reasons for Vladimir's and Estragon's waiting, but this does not interact with the fact that the two characters are physically present there on the country road.

Dante's second meaning is the allegorical one. His allegory is based on Christian Revelation; the Hebrews became free through their escape from Egypt, in the same way as people are saved by the birth of Christ. From the point of view of an author of literature, Dante considers the birth of Christ as the event that enables him to complete with a Christian significance the stylistic perfection of classical authors.

An ideal aim is not so easy to find in Beckett. He wants to create something new, as stated in the already quoted first of the *Three Dialogues*: "Yet I speak of an art turning from it [the feasible] in disgust, weary of its puny exploits, weary of pretending to be able, of being able, of doing a little better the same old thing, of going a little further along a dreary road." (139) Beckett is not looking for a variation in the expression of a subject, he is looking for a new way of expressing a completely new subject. Beckett's allegory can thus be considered as a manifestation of the need to find something totally different from what has been said up to that moment, and to be able to express it in a new way. It is not a correction, an enrichment, an explanation of a hidden language like Dante's; it is a destruction, an attempt to leave behind whatever has been said and which has used up its power of communication and has transformed itself into "the same old thing". If Dante recognises the stylistic perfection of classical poets, Beckett does not have any more examples to follow. He is creating his own way and his own new subject(s). It is the destruction of the second level of meaning; after the literal, also the allegorical is transformed into nonsense.

At least, apparently. Coming back to the trilogy, we can find an allegorical meaning, namely the fact that the characters are looking for something, they are carrying on a search. Molloy is looking for his mother, Moran is searching for Molloy and is trying to understand the voice he hears. Malone is looking for death, and the unnamable is searching for something that he cannot give up searching for, something he cannot fully grasp with his mind (cf. Part III, where I will deal with the unnamable's logic and the reasons for its defeat). This quest of the four characters is Beckett's allegory of the need to look for new subjects and new mechanisms.

The unnamable is the quintessence of Beckett's allegorical sense; he incarnates the final defeat of rationality as an omnicomprehensive method in order to understand the human psyche and the complexity of the cosmos. Beckett's redemption (Dante describes the allegorical meaning of his example as the fact that we have been redeemed by Christ) is that he has inwardly felt this irrational and universal feeling of chaos and that he has to describe it. The unnamable is a character born of Beckett's need to destroy whatever may already have been expressed, because Beckett feels that all the ways of logical expression used up to that moment are insufficient to allow him to approach what he is looking for.

Dante's third meaning is the moral one. Dante describes it as the passage of the soul from the darkness and sadness of sin to a state of grace. The moral meaning of the trilogy is that of a passage from a physical search (Molloy, Moran) to a psychological one (Moran, Malone) and finally to a spiritual one (the unnamable's silence). The fact that at the end of *The Unnamable*, Beckett is still searching, shows the importance of the mechanism of the search and the inconsistency of the results.

The fourth meaning is the anagogic one. Dante referring to his example describes it as the passage of the blessed soul from the slavery of earthly corruption to the freedom of eternal glory. The anagogic meaning of the trilogy deals with the mechanism which shows that leaning on the rational part of man only salvation (the final "to go silent" of the unnamable) is impossible to achieve.

To sum up. Beckett's problems, in the quintessence of the unnamable, are created by his need for something and by his not being able to achieve it. The unnamable refers to that something as the ability to fall silent. Trying to become silent, he speaks continuously of his inability to stop talking. Sentences like "Nothing ever troubles me. And yet I am troubled." (269) show that his existential system lacks something important. This lacking part should compensate for the unnamable's rambling mind; it should enable him to clarify what is unexpressed in his speech, which "will never utter affirmations nor negations without invalidating them, or sooner or later." (267) If the literal sense of the novel refers to the unnamable's mind and to its creation (which should be rational but cannot be because it tries to describe something which is beyond its reach, and which thus destroys everything, itself included, giving an impression of nonsense), the allegorical one deals with Beckett's unexpressed spiritual part. This unexpressed part is the subject of the three allegorical meanings, its existence, its ties with the rational, and its essentiality.

The second element mentioned by Dante is the "agens". "Agens igitur [...] est ille qui dictus est [i.e. Dante the Pilgrim], et totaliter videtur esse." (624) The agent is the character who performs the action described in the poetical text. In the *Comedy* it is Dante the Pilgrim who, led first by Virgil and then by Beatrice, walks through the three kingdoms where dead people receive what they have deserved by their actions during their lives. In the course of his ascent, Dante undergoes a major change, from doubtful to faithful, from being a sinner to a state of enlightenment. In the trilogy we have something similar. But before I start to describe the similarities between Beckett and Dante, it is necessary to spend a few words on the trilogy's narrator. Dina Sherzer writes:

> Tout d'abord nous parlons d'un narrateur, mais n'y a-t-il pas plusieurs narrateurs qui prennent la parole successivement? Dans chaque roman celui qui parle s'exprime à la première personne, et nous pourrions penser que le 'je' est un *embrayeur* (Jakobson, 1963) qui renvoie dans la première partie de *Molloy*, à un narrateur s'appelant Molloy, dans la deuxième partie à un narrateur s'appelant Moran, dans *Malone meurt* à un narrateur s'appelant Malone, et dans *L'Innomable* à un narrateur qui n'a pas de nom. Mais nous nous apercevons vite que d'abord, le nom, quand il y en a un, figure dans le titre et n'est que rarement employé dans le cours du texte lui-même, et ensuite, qu'en fin de compte, il s'agit toujours du même narrateur qui emploie les mêmes procédés et adopte les mêmes attitudes de livre en livre. (15)

If considering the four narrators as a single person is exaggerated, it is certainly true that they employ the same methods and they have the same attitudes. We can, de facto, consider them as a single narrator (from here on the Narrator) because the (literal) destructive force and the (allegorical) spiritual sense of looking for something, which are the 'engine' of their words, are to be found throughout the four parts, and although constantly developing, are one and the same. The trilogy presents one agent who undergoes several changes in the course of the narration, the gradual loss of mobility, the continuous fading of coherence, the destruction of the syntax. These

Part II – "The Nothing with which to express and the Nothing from which to express"

themes will be dealt with thoroughly in Part III, but a first conclusion can be drawn here. Beckett's Narrator is an "agens" i.e. a person who performs an action. The action's tasks are ordered in an ascending climax from physical to abstract. Molloy acts in order to reach his mother's house (totally physical, Molloy's relationship with his mother is also completely based on physical contact); Moran starts by acting in order to find Molloy (physical journey to Ballybaba), and ends up searching for the speaking voice (abstract journey to his conscience); Malone looks for death (physical and abstract end); and the unnamable looks for silence (abstract end, death having failed to bring peace). The Narrator aims at a definitive status which could solve his problems. There is an ascending climax in the intensity and spirituality of this aspiration; Molloy could stop rambling, Moran could go back home (finding Molloy) and find out what he does not understand (being able to decipher the voice), Malone could stop writing his stories and his comments, and the unnamable could stop thinking and hearing. The Narrator's actions are similar to those of the fictional pilgrim of Dante. The pilgrim (*Inf.* i, 2-3) is travelling in the underworld because he has found himself in a "selva oscura / che la dritta via era smarrita" (Gloomy wood, astray / Gone from the path direct). He is in a state of confusion, and he has to pass through Hell and Purgatory to gain his bliss again in the experience of Paradise. Beckett's Narrator has to bear the burden of irrational actions which lead to the complete silence of rationality in order to find his "dritta via". Dante succeeds (when he has the vision of God); the Narrator, at the end of *The Unnamable*, is still searching for his allegorical realisation. But, as already mentioned, what is important is his looking for something. As we will see in Part II, Ch. 2., Beckett concentrates on Hell and Purgatory, and his characters never reach Dante's Eden and Paradise.

The third element mentioned by Dante Alighieri is the structure.

Forma vero est duplex: forma tractatus et forma

tractandi. Forma tractatus est triplex, secundum triplicem divisionem. Prima divisio est, qua totum opus dividitur in tres canticas. Secunda, qua quelibet cantica dividitur in cantus. Tertia, qua quilibet cantus dividitur in rithimos. Forma sive modus tractandi est poeticus, fictivus, descriptivus, digressivus, transumptivus, et cum hoc diffinitivus, divisivus, probativus, improbativus, et exemplorum positivus. (612-4)

The structure is double: the structure of the work and the structure of the contents. The structure of the work is triple, following a triple subdivision. The first one is that the text is subdivided into parts; the second that each part is subdivided into cantos; and the third that each canto is subdivided into rhythms. The structure or way in which the contents are treated is poetic, fictive, descriptive, digressive, summarising, and at the same time definitive, dividing, probating, non probating and illustrative. (my translation)

Dante's " forma" is double; it consists of the "forma tractatus" and of the "forma tractandi". The "forma tractatus" i.e. the structure of the *Comedy* is triple, following a triple subdivision. The first one is that the text is subdivided into parts; the second that each part is subdivided into cantos; and the third that each canto is subdivided into rhythms. Dante is very precise in defining structures, because he thinks an ordered text hints at the divine order that rules the universe. Beckett does not order his texts rationally because, as stated in *Three Dialogues*, he does not believe that such an order is positive. "My case, since I am in the dock, is that van Velde is the first to desist from this estheticized automatism [representation], the first to admit that to be an artist is to fail" (145). Beckett considers the structure a hindrance; he calls it "estheticized automatism" because, he claims,

Part II – "The Nothing with which to express and the Nothing from which to express"

artists have always thought of the structure as something that should represent the world's beauty and perfection. To give a structure to a work implies that the author knows where he wants to start, what he wants to say and where he wants to stop. Beckett has no idea; he refuses to know where he should start or end his narrative and what it should be about. The trilogy is an example of this lack of structure. Molloy's narration is divided into two paragraphs only; Moran's story seems to start with a stylistic order, but soon loses it; Malone at the beginning explains what he wants to say, but then changes his mind; and the unnamable has neither a program nor a structure and his narration is, after a short introduction, a single paragraph which contains sentences that go on for pages. Neither Molloy's nor Moran's nor Malone's nor the unnamable's story have a beginning or an ending; they all start at a certain point and end at another (which sometimes is the same one as at the beginning), but no logic links up the two extremities because what is stated at the beginning is not valid anymore at the end. Again Beckett uses a Dantean suggestion to show its unworthiness; Dante's forma becomes Beckett's amoebic structure which swallows up everything to spit it out chewed and completely unrecognisable.

The structure of the "forma tractandi" i.e. the form of the contents, is described by Dante as poetic, fictive, descriptive, digressive, summarising, and at the same time definitive, dividing, probating, non probating and illustrative. Dante uses many terms to point out the various ways of expression used in the *Comedy*. It is not necessary to enter into the details of that list. Its being so long demonstrates that Dante has a wide concept of the structures the "forma tractandi" can take. Dante comments on his list saying that all these structures have the aim of hiding theological truths by means of fictive reality. Again we see that there is a negative relation between Dante and Beckett. Beckett is not interested in hiding Truth; if it exists, and if it could be told, it is already hidden from his comprehension. Beckett's "forma tractandi" has no structure because he is confronted with an amount of material which he is unable to cope with and to order in a structure. Beckett uses structures to underline the vacuity of the words contained in them. If Dante's structure is positive and it underlines the positive ideas which it contains, Beckett's is non-existent and underlines the annihilation of meaning.

The fourth element Dante considers important for the comprehension of a doctrinal work is the "finis" or "utilitas" or "causa finalis".

> Finis totius et partis esse posset et multiplex, scilicet propinquus et remotus; sed, omissa subtili investigatione, dicendum est breviter quod finis totius et partis est removere viventes in hac vita de statu miserie et perducere ad statum felicitatis. (624)

> The aim of the whole work [i.e. the *Comedy*] and of its third part [i.e. *Paradise*] could be multiple i.e. near or far away. But it could be possible to claim that the aim of the whole work and of this part is to move the souls of sinners away from misery and lead them to bliss. (my translation)

The aim of Dante's *Comedy* is to move the souls of sinners away from misery and lead them to bliss. As we have seen, Dante hides this truth by the fictive reality of his journey in the underworld. He does not directly state, in his work, that he wants to convert people to a righteous life. He presents (the status of) people who have behaved in different ways, leaving to the reader the freedom to decide how to act.[26] Beckett's declared purpose is to show that there is nothing to express and nothing with which to express it. An example. In the trilogy the Narrator presents his world of confusion and noise. He affirms again and again that nothing true will be said in the narration because he does not know what truth is, and that if he suspects he has spoken it,

Part II – "The Nothing with which to express and the Nothing from which to express"

he will say the contrary and then negate everything. We know that Beckett wants to create a kind of art which is completely new, but that he does not know how to do it, or wants to create it in its negation. His aim is to show that an aim does not exist.

Beckett's "causa finalis" has to be considered as his attempt to find a new way of communication by destroying what he considers to be of no use to him in his aim or in the affirmation of a total lack of possibility of communication.

The fifth element mentioned by Dante is the title of the book, "libri titulus" or "inscription".

> Libri titulus est: "Incipit Comedia Dantis Alagherii, florentini natione, non moribus". Ad cuius notitiam sciendum est quod comedia dicitur a "comos" villa et "oda" quod est cantus, unde comedia quasi "villanus cantus". (614)

> The title of the book is "Here begins the Comedy of Dante Alighieri, born in Florence but who does not accept what is happening in the city." To understand the title it is necessary to know that the word "comedy" stems from the word "comos" which means "village" and from the word "oda" which means "song". Thus "comedy" almost means "sung in a village". (my translation)

Dante chooses to write a comedy (instead of a tragedy) for three reasons. The first one, mentioned in his *Epistola*, is that "comedia vero inchoat asperitatem alicuius rei, sed eius materia prospere terminator" (616-8), while a tragedy "in principio est admirabilis et quieta, in fine seu exitu est fetida et horribilis" (614-6). It is typical of the Christian mentality to give priority to a situation which at its beginning is problematic but ends joyfully because it is similar to Christ's death and resurrection and to the passage of souls from sin to bliss. A second reason is that classical theories consider tragedies to be of greater value than comedies because tragedies deal with serious matters while comedies deal with trifling ones. Dante, who considers himself superior to classical authors, has chosen to write a comedy in order to show that his superiority relates not only to contents but also to stylistic features, and he can thus choose the style he prefers. Alighieri's choosing to write a comedy can be explained by the similarity between his comical structure and the spiritual path of Christianity, and by Dante's feeling superior to classical authors.

Beckett's writings are structured in a similar way.[27] He has built up his own personal style, which is a mixture of classical and popular ones (tragic, comic, picaresque, etc.). His style is the result of his ideas and convictions; he thinks that every established kind of expression is inadequate. Thus his works constantly diminish language. Moreover he feels that the human mind on its own is a restless and useless instrument, so that his works describe the defeat of rationality. Beckett's view of the world is transformed in his poetry, but not being able to identify with any of the existing styles, he has to invent his own. We do not know if Beckett considers himself superior to his contemporaries and to the tradition he is compared with, but it is certainly true that he does not consider himself part of them and that he feels he has to discover new ways of expression to replace the old ones and not be superimposed on them, as is the case with Dante.

The third reason why Dante chose to compose a comedy and not a tragedy is that there is a difference of language. "Similiter differunt in modo loquendi: elate et sublime tragedia; comedia vero remisse et humiliter." (618) And about the language of the comedy he writes "ad modum loquendi, remissus est modus et humilis, quia locutio vulgaris in qua et muliercule comunicant." (620-2) Although the poetical language was still Latin, Dante wrote his *Comedy* in Vulgar Italian because he wanted to reach a wider audience. Beckett's linguistic choice was also intended to substitute the existing use of language, but from another point of view it is innovative if compared to Dante's. In fact, Beckett's language was not chosen to involve a group of existing people, but to create a new kind of people. Dante's use of language aims at unifying Italic regions, Beckett's aims at unifying single persons that feel the importance of the problems he is concerned with, which have to be sensed between the lines because of his annihilation of language.

Beckett, destroying grammatical, syntactic, lexical rules and meaning, creates a sort of non-language (or rather, a way of expression which is to a certain extent not subject to conventional rules). His readers cannot be conventional either; they have to interpret the text at different levels from the lexical to the allegorical. This means that Beckett's works are unitive for those readers who are looking for what Beckett tries to say, readers who are patient and constant. Beckett's works create and unite a new kind of reader, a person searching at all levels who is also open to failure.

The sixth and last element mentioned by Dante is the "genus phylosophie". "Genus vero phylosophie sub quo hic in toto et parte proceditur, est morale negotium, sive ethica; quia non ad speculandum, sed ad opus inventum est totum et pars." (624) Dante claims that his work was conceived for action and not for philosophical speculation. Beckett's poetry was written for action too, but of a different kind. Dante means action in life in order to earn God's final approval, Beckett's action is that of searching for and understanding in his texts, the voice of the Muse. As already seen in the chapter on Plato, they both have been forced to write, Dante by Truth, Beckett by the need to express.

To summarise. Applying some elements of Dante Alighieri's view of poetry, we have seen that Samuel Beckett's works are an attempt to create a new way of expression. We have considered this mechanism and we have concluded that it has a dual objective. Beckett wants to destroy traditional rules and in this destruction he wants to find the force to make him write, or at least he wants to hint at the fact that he has to look for it. This aim is also explained in the description of Beckett's subject; his characters, with their endless speeches, look for a definitive solution to their problems. Beckett's literal sense copes with the destruction of traditional rules, while the allegorical one hints at the spiritual part which should rise (but, in fact, does not) from its ashes. We have seen that Beckett speaks of characters and structures which try to describe the madness of a rationality which deals only with itself, not considering its spiritual counterpart. When dealing with Dante's "inscription" we have seen how Beckett organises his work. His refusal to accept a particular classical or established style has caused him to mix them all together and filter them through his psyche, obtaining a new product which has little (and does not want to have anything) in common with its components. We have then sketched an outline of Beckett's ideal reader; he or she is a person who, spurred on by his or her intuition that something important is to be found between the lines in Beckett's works, searches at all its levels. He or she starts with the literal one and, overcoming the destructive difficulties of this level, goes on to the allegorical and spiritual ones. Finally, we have considered the "genus phylosophie" of Beckett's poetry, concluding that his works are designed to understand a spiritual truth.

Dante's Superiority Over the Classics

Another interesting opinion of Dante to be discussed is that Christian literature is superior to classical literature. As we have seen, Dante considers classical authors to be the greatest authorities on style but cannot totally approve of the contents of their poems because they were written before Christ's birth, and thus lack His Revelation. Dante considers himself as the poet who transforms these pagan works into Christian Truths. Like Christ, who has come and has fulfilled the sayings of previous prophets, Dante, by writing his *Comedy*, wants to give a religious sense to all these works. Dante is the last great medieval writer; the following generation, and Petrarca is its main exponent, was already different. Francesco Petrarca was the first poet to suggest a humanistic view of classical authors. Petrarch is thus not writing poetry in order to conclude a cycle with a perfect work inspired by God himself; he is conscious of the imperfection of his works and of the necessity for continuous revision. An example is his *Canzoniere*, which he started revising in 1342 and stopped on the 18th of July 1374, the day of his death. Petrarca is useful in that he helps us to place Dante in a system of considering progress in literature. Dante's definitive writings are soon overwhelmed by a sense of insecurity in what has been written. Beckett can be placed in between these two positions; on the one hand he is the apex of a cultural development and the voice that connects and gives a sense to its parts; on the other hand, he is the creator of a new way of considering art and an exponent who describes the imperfection and precariousness of a literary text.

Beckett used nearly every writing form, showing his interest for self-renewal. He wrote novels, short stories, poems, plays, screenplays, pieces for radio. He translated them from French to English and vice versa, he actively took part in rehearsals in French, English and German. His activities tended to cover all literary levels (composition, form, translation, mise-en-scene) and of all media (magazine, book, theatre, television, radio). The contents of his works deal with universal principles. What are human beings born for? Why do they have to live? How do they have to live? Is it possible to be happy? Is there a sense in life? On giving a structure to his works and to their contents, Beckett does not develop any existing theory or form; he unifies them but brings them to a critical point. He shows that they are useless and cannot be improved unless by negating them, and by negating that negation. The sense that he gives to the cultural development he dominates is that it has exhausted its force and in order to give continuity to it he has to destroy it. He uses existing forms because there are no others, but he uses them to show their uselessness and the need for completely different ones. This is where he comes close to Petrarch. There is a gradual shift of importance away from a religious view of the world towards a humanistic one. Beckett does not write because he is interested in the future of humanity and wants to improve its morality (like Dante), but because he feels the presence of these problems goading him and he tries to get rid of them by writing.

What is Petrarch's attitude towards writing? In his *Secretum*, Francesco (a personification of the normal part of Petrarca's intelligence) is accused by Agostino (the most critical part of his intelligence) of being too proud of his rationality, culture and literary ability. Francesco answers:

> Me ne fisum ais ingenio? At profecto nullum ingenioli mei signum est, nisi hoc unum, nullam me in eo posuisse fiduciam. Ego ne librorum ex lectione superbior fiam, que michi sicut scientie modicum invexit, sic curarum materiam multarum? An lingue gloriam sectatus dicor qui, ut tu ipse memorasti, nichil magis indigner, quam conceptibus illam meis non posse sufficere? (78)

> You claim that I boast about my genius? But if I can be considered a genius it is only because I have never used that talent. I spend much time reading, and from this occupation I have gained much more pain than knowledge. And you accuse me of enjoying the glory of language; but you too have admitted that I am afflicted by my inability to describe the concepts I am concerned with. (my translation)

Petrarca claims that if there has been any genius (ingenio) in his life, he has not relied on it. He then adds that from his rationality and his culture he has gained more pain than knowledge. And, he concludes, he has been accused too long of enjoying the glory of language, but in reality he is afflicted by its inability to describe the concepts he is concerned with. Petrarch, in contrast to Dante, feels the insufficiency of his human and rational part, of his language and of his culture. He understands that they are not enough to enable him to grasp those concepts that he wants to express. We notice how Petrarch and Beckett have similar attitudes towards writing; they both see that language cannot fully describe what they need to say, they both seem resigned to accept the defeat of their rationality. There is only one major difference.

> Petrarch was too intelligent not to have realized the exceptional quality of his own gifts; but he was also constantly aware of his limitations. [...] But such pride as he had was tempered both by a harassing sense of insufficiencies and by recognition of the abilities that he possessed as being gifts bestowed upon him rather than achievements of his own. (Wilkins, 256-7)

Petrarch is conscious of his limits and he knows that his qualities cannot solve his problems but he is also aware that his abilities come from somewhere else and not from himself. Beckett too, sees the limits of his rationality but does not accept its defeat. He constantly concentrates on that topic, and he does so by writing about his rationality's defeat, using his literary qualities to describe it. The incomprehension of the origin of his abilities and of their mechanism, forces Beckett to search his mind for something he cannot grasp through his rationality. His search is a vicious circle; he is condemned to failure.

Dante, Petrarca and Beckett are well aware of their qualities. Dante and Beckett use them in a similar way in that they try to create something that should revolutionise what already exists. But Petrarca and Beckett are also well aware of their limits, and it is here that they approach, both their works deal with that limit.

Belacqua and "Colui che fece per viltà il gran rifiuto" (*Inf.*, iii, 59-60)

Dante's *Inferno* and *Purgatorio* have been demonstrated to attract Beckett very much. As already seen, Beckett fills the trilogy with images taken from Dante's first two canticles, and their atmosphere permeates his work. This sub-chapter will concentrate on two episodes taken from Dante's *Commedia*: the one about Belacqua (*Purg.*, iv, 88-139), and the infernal limbo (*Inf.*, iii, 22-69). Both episodes are particular in that they take place outside the reign they belong to; the first one occurs in the Ante-Purgatorio, and the second in the Ante-Inferno. Beckett's trilogy can be described as taking inspiration from both Dante's *Inferno* and *Purgatorio*, but it can be claimed that *Molloy* and *Malone Dies* are near to a purgatorial view (in that Molloy, Moran and Malone are hoping for something), while *The Unnamable* is more infernal (we are presented with a total standstill, where nothing can be hoped for anymore). In this sub-chapter we will consider some more similarities between these two episodes and the trilogy, remembering that we are not trying to place Molloy, Moran and Malone in Purgatory nor the unnamable in Hell, but that we are hinting at that possibility remembering that there are many other ones.

The infernal limbo is the first place Dante the Pilgrim and Virgil encounter in their journey through Hell. Entering it, they leave the light of the sun, and try to regain it by passing through Hell. At the beginning of Purgatory, Dante the Pilgrim and Virgil see again the sun and feel the fresh air after having resided in the miasmas of Hell. The two episodes thus witness the beginning and the end of

Part II – "The Nothing with which to express and the Nothing from which to express"

Dante's deep despair because of his leaving earthly and heavenly lights. Molloy's and Moran's journeys take place in the country of Ballybaba; the unusual natural setting for Beckett can be considered as an allusion to both the "selva oscura" (*Inf.*, i, 2) where the *Comedy* begins, and where Dante loses the right way, and to the Pilgrim's "uscimmo a riveder le stele" (*Inf.*, xxxiv, 139), when he sees the stars at the end of Hell and finds himself on the beach at the bottom of the purgatorial mountain.

It is not far from the bottom of Purgatory that the episode of Belacqua takes place. Many surveys have concentrated on the encounter between Dante and Belacqua, and its intertextual dialogue with Beckett, but two things have not yet been stressed enough in this episode, Belacqua's transitory state and the allegory his character suggests. The episode begins with Virgil's geographical explanation of Purgatory and Belacqua's ironic comment.[28]

> "[...] Questa montagna è tale,
> che sempre al cominciar di sotto è grave;
> e quant'uom più va su, e men fa male.
> Però quand'ella ti parrà soave
> tanto, che su andar ti fia leggero
> com'a seconda giù andar per nave,
> allor sarai al fin d'esto sentero:
> quivi di riposar l'affanno aspetta.
> Più non rispondo e questo so per vero".
> E com'elli ebbe sua parola detta,
> una voce di presso sonò: "Forse
> che di sedere in pria avrai distretta!" (*Purgatorio*, iv, 88-99)[29]

Virgil's description of the ascent of the mountain of Purgatory ("Such is this steep ascent, / That it is ever difficult at first, / But more a man proceeds, less evil grows") is parodied by the descending climax of Molloy's difficulty in moving and the fact that his inability to move does not get better as he, and the trilogy, go on. Molloy's crawls in the forest at the end of the novel, Moran's knee hurts and he is not able to move anymore, Malone is immobile. Belacqua's (but it could be Dante's) instinctive and sudden answer, which reminds Dante's human body that needs to take a rest, presents two inclinations well known to Molloy, Moran and Malone, the ideal need to do something (visit his mother, find Molloy, die) and the possibility of not being able to achieve that task, mixed with a subtle and apathetic irony which underlines the possibility of a change of mind. Molloy, Moran, Malone and Belacqua are similar; they are all waiting for something which does not depend on them.

Molloy, at the beginning of the trilogy, is even sitting in the same foetal position as Belacqua.

> I was perched higher than the road's highest point and flattened what is more against a rock the same colour as myself, that is grey. The rock he probably saw. He gazed around as if to engrave the landmarks on his memory and must have seen the rock in the shadow of which I crouched like Belacqua, or Sordello, I forget. (*Molloy*, 12)[30]

> Al suon di lei ciascun di noi si torse,
> e vedemmo a mancina un gran petrone,
> del qual né io né ei prima s'accorse.
> Là ci traemmo; ed ivi eran persone
> che si stavano all'ombra dietro al sasso
> come l'uom per negghienza a star si pone.
> E un dir lor, che mi sembiava lasso,
> sedeva e abbracciava le ginocchia,
> tenendo il viso giù tra esse basso. (iv, 100-108)[31]

Molloy and Belacqua both sit higher than the road they are looking

Part II – "The Nothing with which to express and the Nothing from which to express"

at, and on which someone is walking (the man known as C in *Molloy*, Dante the Pilgrim and Virgil in the *Comedy*); they both lie against a big rock; they both sit in the shadow and they both are crouched; they are both unseen.

Beckett is conscious that Dante's Ante-Purgatory is a place remarkably different from what precedes it (i.e. Hell) and what follows it (Purgatory and Heaven), and that here reigns a sort of harmonious stasis. In fact Beckett noticed that here we have for the first time in the *Comedy* a high concentration of smiles, something brought to light by Mary Bryden, in her article "Beckett and the Three Dantean Smiles". Bryden describes three undated hand-written postcards which accompanied the editions of *The Divine Comedy* which Beckett donated to Reading University Library. Let us consider what Bryden writes about Dante's smile to Belacqua:

> Beckett demonstrates in his postcard notes a sensitivity to the more lighthearted moments of the Ante-Purgatorial journey. He is particularly absorbed by the smiles to be found there, and notes down three of them. [...]
>
> The third smile registered by Beckett is in Canto 4, line 122. The first two smiles have been bestowed upon Dante by shades. This one, however, appears on the Pilgrim's own face, prompted by his unexpected meeting with the lounging Belacqua, and here Beckett jots down: "Dante smiles (at Belacqua). D's first smile?" This smile is of a rather different quality from the others. First, it is a passing glimmer rather than a broad smile: "mosson le labbra mie un poco a riso" (made me half smile). Secondly, its significance extends further than the welcoming courtesy which had characterized the first two smiles. Dante's old friend Belacqua has been listening unseen to the earnest disquisition given by Virgil in response to Dante's question about the

position of the sun. When Dante finally moves into view, Belacqua stirs his lethargic pose just sufficiently to ask sarcastically: "It is quite clear to you by now / just why the sun drives past you on the left? (lines 119-20)[32] (30-1)

That to Belacqua is, in fact, Dante's first smile. Beckett notices this situation and translates it into the opening scene of Molloy. But why does Dante smile? It has been suggested that his half smile is caused by sarcasm, but it is probably not the case. Dante smiles because of Belacqua's lazy movements and his brief words, and not because of irony: "Li atti suoi pigri e le corte parole / mosser le labbra mie un poco a riso" (His lazy acts and broken words my lips / To laughter somewhat moved, iv, 121-2). Belacqua's appearance causes in Dante a series of uncontrolled moods, from comic to melancholic to reflective, from a parable (Belacqua symbolising human fragility in contrast with Virgil's ideal impetus of the soul) to a spirit of indulgence (Dante smiles because he is happy to find his friend Belacqua there). It is in these mixed feelings and in the dichotomy ideal impetus of the soul versus the fragility and irony of the flesh, that we find Beckett's primary interest in this episode and for the Ante-Purgatory in general.

Dante's physical description of how Belacqua is sitting may have inspired Beckett in his description of Molloy, but what seems to fascinates Beckett most is, once again, a mechanism. In *Molloy* and *Malone Dies* we can find both Belacqua's inactivity (Molloy, Moran, Malone and Belacqua are, at some stage, prevented from moving), and Virgil's impetuous need to move towards the aim he wants to achieve (Virgil wants to reach Purgatory's doors, Molloy is pushed to look for his mother, Moran looks for Molloy, Malone wants to die). Belacqua's longing for Purgatory and salvation becomes Molloy's need to reach his town and his mother's room, Moran's trying to understand the voice he hears, and Malone's longing for death; Belacqua's laziness, as already seen, is transformed into Molloy's, Moran's and Malone's impossibility to move. What is missing in Beckett is the presence of divine order, and this causes Belacqua's needs to become earthly and material in the characters of the trilogy.

The encounter of the Pilgrim with Belacqua, although they were friends, lacks the impetus one would expect, but this is due to Belacqua's lazy attitude towards life, which seem to involve Dante, who nevertheless is tired of walking up the steep mountain. Belacqua's laziness, Dante seems to suggest, is more involving than Virgil's impetus; Molloy's forgetting to look for his mother and his "destruction" of Moran could be seen as a parody of this episode.

Belacqua's fear is not that of being forever exiled or excluded from Purgatory, and later from the vision of God; he knows that he will be admitted to Purgatory and he longs for his punishments. Belacqua is sitting outside Purgatory for an amount of time as long as his life on earth: "Prima convien che tanto il ciel m'aggiri / di fuor da essa, quanto fece in vita" (Behoves so long that Heaven first bear me round / Without its limits, as in life it bore, iv, 130-1). Belacqua knows that his waiting will have an end, and that he will be admitted to his punishment first, and finally to the vision of God. What he fears is to be forgotten on earth, and this because if someone prays for his soul, he will have to wait less outside Purgatory: "se orazion in prima non m'aita / che surga su di cuor che in grazia viva" (iv, 133-4).[33] These verses show what Belacqua really cares about; he wants someone to pray to God for him because his own prayers are not listened to in Heaven. God and his mercy are parodied by Beckett in Molloy's and Moran's failing and in Moran's trust for something superior that in the end he does not understand and which disappoints him (Youdi's words about life being "a thing of beauty and a joy forever" 151; God, who begins to disgust Moran). Beckett's characters do not have Belacqua's hope, or better, Molloy hopes to find his mother and Moran hopes to find Molloy, but they both do not know if they will succeed and eventually fail.³⁴

After Malone's "death", Beckett's writing takes more inspiration from Dante's Hell. *The Unnamable* is an infernal novel; its places and characters are endlessly condemned to the circularity of their own words and images. It is at the beginning of the unnamable's account that we have to leave the episode of Belacqua and go back to Hell and more precisely to the Ante-Inferno. Again a place which is still not included in the reign it precedes. As soon as Dante and Virgil enter Hell, passing beneath the words "lasciate ogni speranza, voi ch'entrate" (*Inf.*, iii, 9), they find themselves in the Ante-Inferno.³⁵

> Quivi sospiri, pianti e alti guai   22
> risonavan per l'aere sanza stelle,
> per ch'io al cominciar ne lagrimai.
> Diverse lingue, orribili favelle,   25
> parole di dolore, accenti d'ira,
> voci alte e fioche, e suon di man con elle
> facevano un tumulto, il qual s'aggira   28
> sempre in quell'aura sanza tempo tinta,
> come la rena quando turbo spira.³⁶

The place is remarkably similar to the unnamable's "here". Both places are dark (Dante's "air pierced by no star", and the unnamable's "[c]lose to me it is grey, dimly transparent, and beyond that charmed circle deepens and spreads its fine impenetrable veils" 275); the movement inside it is circular (Dante's "tumulto qual s'aggira", and the unnamable's description of the collision between two shapes, 272).

> E io ch'avea d'orror la testa cinta,   31
> dissi: "Maestro, che è quel ch'i' odo?

> e che gent'è che par nel duol sì vinta?"
> Ed elli a me: "Questo misero modo 34
> tengon l'anime triste di coloro
> che visser sanza infamia e sanza lodo.
> Mischiate sono a quel cattivo coro 37
> delli angeli che non furon ribelli
> né pur fedeli a Dio, ma per sé foro.
> Caccianli i ciel per non esser men belli, 40
> né lo profondo inferno li riceve,
> ch'alcuna gloria i rei avrebber d'elli".
> E io: "Maestro, che è tanto greve 43
> a lor, che lamentar li fa sì forte?"
> Rispuose: "Dicerolti molto breve.
> Questi non hanno speranza di morte, 46
> e la loro cieca vita è tanto bassa,
> che 'nvidiosi son d'ogni altra sorte.
> Fama di loro il mondo esser non lassa; 49
> misericordia e giustizia li sdegna:
> non ragioniam di loro, ma guarda e passa."[37]

The souls in Dante's limbo are described as having "lived / Without or praise or blame", and the unnamable often claims never to have taken up a position in any debate whatsoever. The two creatures he invents, Mahood and Worm, are not noticed by anyone (Mahood) or do not exist (Worm). Virgil claims that "These of death / No hope may entertain" and Dante writes that "these wretches [...] ne'er lived". This reminds us of the unnamable's continuously being aware of his eternity and of his never having lived.

> E io, che riguardai, vidi una insegna 52
> che girando correva tanto ratta,
> che d'ogni posa mi pareva indegna;
> e dietro le venia sì lunga tratta 55

> di gente, ch'io non averei creduto
> che morte tanta n'avesse disfatta.
> Poscia che io v'ebbi alcun riconosciuto,   58
> vidi e riconobbi l'ombra di colui
> che fece per viltà il gran rifiuto.[38]
> Incontanente inteso e certo fui   61
> che questa era la setta de' cattivi,
> a Dio spiacenti ed a' nemici sui.
> Questi sciagurati, che mai non fur vivi,   64
> erano ignudi e stimolati molto
> da mosconi e da vespe ch'eran ivi.
> Elle rigavan lor di sangue il volto,   67
> che, mischiato di lagrime, ai lor piedi
> da fastidiosi vermi era ricolto. (iii, 22-69)[39]

Dante says that he "should ne'er / Have thought that death so many had despoiled", and the unnamable claims that "they are all here, at least from Murphy on" (268). All souls have no name and are not recognisable (apart from the one that did the "gran rifiuto"), the unnamable has no name and he forgets other people's names and physiognomies. Dante the Pilgrim, the souls, and the unnamable are weeping. If in the Ante-Purgatory Dante smiles at Belacqua, here he and Virgil disdain the souls they see; the unnamable hates everyone he sees or hears "here". Neither Hell nor Paradise want the inhabitants of the Infernal limbo, and "all other lots / They envy"; the unnamable wants something that he will never be able to achieve.

    The trilogy moves towards a standstill in that the unnamable is excluded (and excludes himself) from whatever may stand outside "here". "I alone am man and all the rest divine" (275). The unnamable's limbo is even more terrible than Dante's, where the damned run behind a destroyed flag without considering what they are doing. The unnamable is forced to think and consider what goes on "there", but he would like not to. If Dante has Virgil who explains to him where they are and what is happening, the unnamable is left in ignorance and even led to confusion by "them".

The Unnamable is not a parody of the Ante-Inferno, as *Molloy* and *Malone Dies* may sometimes be of Belacqua's episode. The unnamable falls in the same despair that Dante describes; no hope, no change, envy for whatsoever destiny, no sense at all (in Dante, souls are condemned to run behind a ridiculous flag; the unnamable is forced to speak without knowing why).

GIAMBATTISTA VICO

This chapter is concerned with Gianbattista Vico's view of history, the role humans have in it, and the development human beings have undergone. The comparison between Beckett and Vico is not to be understood as a comparison of two existing theories: we will apply Vico's theory to Beckett's works, in order to help comprehend Beckett's poetic expression.[40]

A first introductory sub-chapter concentrates on the polemics between Vico and Descartes. On one hand Descartes claims that history cannot be considered a subject for the scientific world, on the other Vico affirms that it is possible to make a science out of it. In his view history is a human product, and thus scientifically demonstrates the evolution of human beings and of society. The following sub-chapters will deal with Vico's way of conceiving history (the distinction between "filosofia" and " filologia"); with the three ages in which Vico divides the development of human society; with Vico's theories on language, poetry and myth; and with the relationship between human beings and history. Finally, Vico's ideas will help us to consider Beckett's trilogy in terms of the division of human society into ages. Worm, the still unborn who does not exist, Molloy, the animistic product of nature, Moran, the product of society, Malone, the end of life, and the unnamable, the limbo inhabitant, are chained one to each other in a similar way to that described by Vico in his "teoria dei corsi e ricorsi storici" (current and recurrent historical ages theory).

The Tension Between Giambattista Vico and René Descartes

It is interesting, before starting to concentrate on Vico's *Scienza Nuova*, to consider the Neapolitan's point of view on Descartes, and see if it can help in our reading of Beckett. In fact, we know that Beckett read and loved Descartes, which he surely already knew in 1930, when he deepened his knowledge of Descartes with Jean Beaufret in Paris (Knowlson, 96-7).[41]

It is exactly in Napoli that, in the second half of the XVIIth century, the first Italian polemics between disciples and opponents of René Descartes took place.[42] Michel Germain (a learned Frenchman) in a letter written in 1685, says: "Descartes a les plus beaux esprits de Naples pour sectateurs. Ils sont avides des ouvrages faits pour sa défense et pour éclaircir sa doctrine." (quoted in Rossi, 10) There is some truth in this. Tommaso Cornelio (1614-1684), mathematician, physician and astronomer, helps to spread Descartes's ideas; Leonardo da Capua, physician and philosopher claims, together with Descartes and Bacon, that modernity is superior to ancient times; Gregorio Caloprese (1650-1715) teaches Descartes's philosophy at university. But on the other hand, there are scholars who dispute Descartes's ideas. The Jesuit De Benedectis accuses Descartes of being a Democritician and Epicurean (and thus an heretic), and Rome bans authors of modern physics such as Galileo, Gassendi and Descartes, because their ideas are "perniciosissime alla repubblica letteraria e alla sincerità della religione." (quoted in Rossi, 9) Giuseppe Valletta, a lawyer writing against De Benedictis's views, summarises the links between the new philosophy and the achievements of science: "essendosi scoperte nuove stelle, nuovi pianeti et altri fenomeni, piante, circolazione di sangue e tante altre cose, e quasi un nuovo mondo, par ch'egli era d'uopo di nuove filosofie per investigarle, non bastando le antiche." (quoted in Rossi, 13) The world is changing, due to scientific, astronomic and anatomical discoveries. And, Valletta claims, it is necessary to have new philosophical ways of analysing these discoveries. It is a dispute between the scientificity of a new view of Nature, and the dogmatic authority of the Church of Rome, which concentrates only on certain aspects of logic and metaphysics.

This, in a nutshell, is the cultural environment in which Giambattista Vico lives and thinks: his *Scienza Nuova*, is not an isolated work, but has to be considered part of this debate.[43] Vico's thought is close to Jesuitical, conservative views; he generally expresses, by means of Christian morality, his disapproval for Descartes's philosophy. But Vico does something more than simply condemn him in a dogmatic way; he describes and discusses Descartes's ideas. Let us consider which ones Vico does not agree with and why. Notice that Beckett considers Vico "as an innovator" ("Dante... Bruno. Vico.. Joyce", 20). In *De nostri temporis studiorum ratione*, Vico analyses the state of scientific study, its relationship with contemporary developments of technique, and the dangers of applying the Descartian analytical method to physics, geometry and medicine. The Neapolitan does not accept the idea of a correspondence between the objective reality of things, and the formal structure of mathematics and geometry. He does not think that a mathematical and geometrical description of the world could be appropriate.

> [M]ethodum geometricam in physicam importarunt, qua veluti Ariadneo aliquo filo alligati, institutum peragunt iter, et caussas, quibus haec admirabilis mundi machina a Deo Opt. Max. constructa est, non iam tentabundi physici, sed velut immensi alicuius operis architecti describunt. (795) [...] At inquiunt docti homines hanc eamdem physicam, qua ipsi methodo docent, ipsam esse naturam: et quoquo te ad universi contemplationem convertas, hanc physicam intueri (803)

New scientists, Vico writes, have transported into physics the geometrical method, and with it they describe the mechanisms of creation. But they describe these mechanisms with a self confidence more appropriate to a supreme and infallible being, rather than to an imperfect product of God. Vico asks who has given those scientists the authority to claim that their "physica" *is* Nature, and he concludes: "ne non tuto iam naturae securi agant: et dum aedium fastigia curant, fundamenta cum periculo negligant. " (803, let us be careful not to treat Nature lightly). Or, in Beckett's words: "God acts on her [Humanity], but by means of her. Humanity is divine, but no man is divine" ("Dante... Bruno. Vico.. Joyce", 22).

But if Vico sets an empirical, Baconian way of knowledge against the Descartian rationality, it is only because at that point of his discourse he can use it to fight Descartes. In fact, about the Baconian idea of human beings dominating the natural world, he writes that

> qui summa tenent, ingentia atque infinita desiderent. Itaque talis in re literalia Verulamius [Bacon] egit, quales in rebus publicis maximorum potentes imperiorum, qui, summam in humanum genus potentiam adepti, ingentes suas opes in ipsam rerum naturam vexare, et sternere saxis maria, velificare montes, aliaque per naturam vetita irrito tamen conati sunt. Enimvero omne, quod homini scire datur, ut et ipse homo, finitum et imperfectum. (*De nostri temporis studiorum ratione*, 791)

Vico claims that the Baconian faith in a science which produces a human being that is able to dominate the world and nature is bizarre, because everything humans happen to know ("omne, quod homini scire datur") is imperfect and partial.

Refusing both the ordering principles of the mathematicians, and the empirical study of the Baconians, Vico places himself outside the contemporary scientific world in a similar way to Beckett in *Three Dialogues*: they both deny the possibility of leaving the impasse in which they have been captured. Vico writes

> [d]emus igitur physicae operam, ut philosophi, nempe ut animum componamus: et in eo praestemus antiquis, quod illi haec studia excolebant, ut impie cum diis de felicitate contenderent; nos autem, ut humanos spiritus deprimamus (*De nostri temporis studiorum ratione*, 803)

Confronted with Nature, in which the mysterious laws of God operate, human beings have to use their knowledge not in order to dominate the world, but in order to become aware of their imperfection. Most interesting is Vico's idea of concentrating on physics with a philosophical eye. In the *Scienza Nuova*, he will paraphrase his own thought by claiming that a human product (history) has to be analysed with a scientific eye (cf. Part II, Ch. 3., the section about "Filosofia" and "Filologia").

There is another major idea of Descartes's philosophy that Vico does not accept, and which is of interest for our understanding of Beckett's work. It is the "cogito ergo sum" theory. Descartes claims that it is possible to doubt the reality of each and every thing in the world, but to do this, the act of thinking is necessary. Thus, thinking is the only certain reality.

> Mais aussitôt après, je pris garde que, pendant que je voulais ainsi penser que tout était faux, il fallait nécessairement que moi, qui le pensais, fusse quelque chose. Et remarquant que cette vérité: *Je pense, donc je suis*, était si ferme et si assurée que toutes les plus extravagantes suppositions des sceptiques n'étaient pas capables de l'ébranler, je jugeai que je pouvais la recevoir sans scruple pour le premier principe de la philosophie que je cherchais. (*Discours de la méthode*, 147-8)

Vico fights this philosophical view. In *De antiquissima Italorum sapientia*, he claims that the human mind can only know the objects that are constructed by thought, and thus he does not accept the "cogito" criterion of reality, because it is not a cognitive act, (it is not science, it does not spread from consciousness itself), but is only a brief moment of awareness.

> Scire enim est tenere genus seu formam, quo res fiat: conscientia autem est eorum, quorum genus seu formam demonstrare non possumus: ita ut passim in vita agenda de rebus, quarum nullum nobis edere signum vel argumentum datur, conscientiam testem demus. (73)

To have consciousness ("conscientia") refers to those things of which we cannot demonstrate the kind nor the shape ("genus seu formam"). It is too easy, Vico adds, to utilise consciousness whenever it is difficult to demonstrate some theory by means of real facts. To know ("scire") means to rebuild an object by passing through a series of connections.

> Scire autem sit rerum elementa componere: unde mentis humanae cogitatio, divinae autem intelligentia sit propria; quod Deus omnia elementa rerum legit, cum extima, tum intima, quia continet et disponit: mens autem humana, quia terminata est, et extra res ceteras omnes, quae ipsa non sunt, rerum duntaxat extrema coactum eat, numquam omnia colligat; ita ut de rebus cogitare quidem possit, intelligere autem non possit; quare particeps sit rationis, non compos. (*De antiquissima Italorum sapientia*, 63)

Humanity can only take part in rationality, but it cannot master it. It may be possible, for human beings, to link some natural events, but this is still far away from a comprehension of the complexity of the entire system. An intuition, Latin *intus-ire* i.e. "to go inside, to understand from inward", is something similar to a sailor, who uses the different kinds of tides, but is not able to describe the forces that produce the movement of the sea.

Beckett inserts himself somewhere in between these points of view; on the one hand he gives great importance to thought, on the other he knows that the act of thinking is useless (Cf. Part I, Ch. 2 on Plato). An example is the unnamable. He literally dwells in mental movement, and shows an awareness of the way in which the process of cognition takes place.

> For to go on means going from here, means finding me, losing me, vanishing and beginning again, a stranger first, then little by little the same as always, in another place, where I shall know nothing, being incapable of seeing, moving, thinking, speaking, but of which little by little, in spite of these handicaps, I shall begin to know something [...] (277).

The unnamable is permeated by a Descartian spirit, but, together with Vico, he also perfectly knows the lack of completeness of thought. "No, I must not think, simply utter." (274) Notwithstanding this, he is not able to avoid the act of thinking. "The compulsion I am under to speak of them, and therefore think of them a little." (276) The unnamable lacks Descartes's optimism about the ability of rationality to clarify the *unknown*. Sum, ergo cogito, seems to suggest the unnamable. Forced by "them", he exists (in his speech); hence the act of thinking. But it seems that the unnamable is the voice of the agony of Descartian rationality, and an admission that Vico is right.

> [H]ere all is strange, all is strange when you come to

> think of it, no, it's coming to think of it that is strange, am I to suppose I am inhabited, I can't suppose anything, I have to go on, that's what I'm doing let others suppose, there must be others in other elsewheres, each one in his little elsewhere, this word that keeps coming back, each one saying to himself, when the moment comes, the moment to say it, Let others suppose, and so on, so on, let others do this, others do that, if there are any, that helps you on, that helps you forward, I believe in progress, I know how to believe too, they must have taught me believing too, no, no one ever taught me anything, I never learnt anything [...] (371).

To the unnamable there remains only what he calls "the spirit of method" (278), or, quoting Descartes,

> [l]a troisième [régle est] de conduire par ordre mes pensées, en commençant par les objets les plus simples et les plus aisés à connaître, pour monter peu à peu, comme par degrés, jusques à la connaissance des plus composés; et supposant même de l'ordre entre ceux qui ne se précèdent point naturellement les uns les autres. (*Discours de la méthode*, 138)

But if the unnamable has no remarkable results, it is because the unnamable knows that what he would like to concentrate on is more than a mere geometrical and rational description, but he is not able to leave a mathematical way of thinking. The unnamable fails because he does not know the objects he is talking about, but nevertheless tries to give a perfect and rational description of them; and because he is not able to understand what he would like.[44]

"Filosofia" and "Filologia": Vico's Way of Conceiving History

In the previous sub-chapter I have described the setting in which Giambattista Vico writes his *Scienza Nuova*, mentioning some of the important polemics between Descartians and anti-Descartians. Now the focus will be shifted on to Vico's major work, but it is important to bear in mind that Beckett knew and loved both Vico and Descartes. The tension between the points of view of these two thinkers has to permeate the reading of this and the three following sub-chapters.

Vico's view of history arises from the joining of universal and particular, abstract and concrete, ideal and factual, or, in his own words, "filosofia" and "filologia". "La filosofia contempla la ragione, onde viene la scienza del vero; la filologia osserva l'autorità dell'umano arbitrio, onde viene la coscienza del certo." (178) Philology has as its object what is certain, while philosophy grasps that truth which is able to explain and justify the "certo". Philology is descriptive, philosophy normative. To produce a result they have to join. Vico wants to be considered the theoretician of these universal rules which may be used to account for the main stages of historic development. Those principles are not *a priori*, but arise from an observation and explanation of historic events, and are used as a way of understanding history. Only in their usefulness do they find their reason for existence. The union of these principles has to undergo a process of judgement by an entire historic age with its customs, political and religious institutions, languages, fairy tales, myths.
Vico describes the role of philosophy as follows.

> La filosofia, per giovare al genere umano, dee sollevare e reggere l'uomo caduto e debole, non convellergli la natura né abbandonarlo alla sua corrozione. [...] La filosofia considera l'uomo quale dev'essere, e sì non può fruttare ch'a pochissimi, che vogliono vivere nella

Part II – "The Nothing with which to express and the Nothing from which to express"

repubblica di Platone, non rovesciarsi nella feccia di Romolo. (175-6)

Philosophy has to help human beings to escape corruption by giving them the strength to considering themselves as they should be.

About "filologia" he writes: "[g]li uomini che non sanno il vero delle cose proccurano d'attenersi al certo, perché, non potendo soddisfare l'intelletto con la scienza, almeno la volontà riposi sulla coscienza" (177-8). Philology too is helpful for humans; it allows them to act in the right way even if they do not understand the theories they should follow. The "certo", what is certain, cannot be considered truth, but has to be considered as a criterion for action. How is it possible to transform philology from being a disconnected series of events into a real science? It is necessary, Vico claims, to discover in it "de' principi della storia ideal eterna, sulla quale corrono in tempo tutte le nazioni ne' loro sorgimenti, progressi, stati decadenze e fini." (206) What is needed is a theoretical framework in which philology has to fit, and this perspective is provided by philosophy. Vico wants to utilise a rule applied in logics ("l'ordine delle idee dee procedere secondo l'ordine delle cose", 204) in the study of history. Philology considers what has been, and is, produced by human communities i.e. all different ways of living, traditions, languages, religious and political institutions. These aspects become real facts only when they are supported by the truth which is shown by philosophy. Truth is the idea (philosophy), certitude is the fact (philology). Truth and certitude have to mingle with each other until they become interchangeable. The aim is to let certitude become truth, and to let truth be verified by certitude. This process transforms the *consciousness* of facts into the *science* of facts.

If it is still premature to look for Beckett's "filosofia" (it is still necessary to consider Vico's in a more careful way), it is nevertheless possible to scan Beckett's trilogy in order to look for its "filologia" i.e. the facts produced by its characters. How do they live? Do they have traditions? What language do they speak? Do they believe in and/or obey some sort of religious or political institutions? Or, speaking more generally, do Molloy, Moran, Malone and the unnamable apply those aspects that Vico considers useful as a way to understand history? Malone and the unnamable are not part of the active world; their stories are not about performances they have accomplished, but invented stories (Malone) or thoughts in the case of the unnamable. From Malone onwards (passing through Mahood and Worm) Beckett seems to have overcome the need for action and any relationship with society. But Molloy and Moran are certainly concerned with many of the aspects applied by Vico; Molloy has to cope with them although he constantly claims that they are useless, Moran, at the beginning of his journey, considers them important, but when he comes back from Ballybaba he thinks they are useless, too. Molloy's way of living is frantic and full of confusion, but it is still organised with a certain order; Molloy has an aim (he has to visit his mother) which he tries to do by walking, cycling or crawling around Ballybaba. He obeys the policeman that stops him (20) and answers the questions of the official at the police station (22), he spends much time in long rituals such as, for example, the stone-sucking episode (64-69) and in creating traditions by recounting episodes from his past. Molloy can express himself but his language is fading.

> I had been living so far from words so long, you understand, that it was enough for me to see my town, since we're talking of my town, to be unable, you understand. It's too difficult to say, for me. And even my sense of identity was wrapped in a namelessness often hard to penetrate, as we have just seen I think. And so on for all the other things which made merry with my senses. Yes, even then, when already all was fading, waves and particles, there could be no things but nameless things, no names but thingless names. I say that

now, but after all what do I know about then, now when the icy words hail down upon me, the icy meanings, and the world dies too, fully named. (30-1)

But even if language fails him (he is generally not understood by his interlocutor), he seems to be able to comprehend what other people say (cf. the episode of the shepherd talking with his dog instead of speaking to him, 28; or Lousse's monologue, 44-5). Furthermore, he finds other ways of communicating e.g. he knocks on his mother skull (18). Molloy knows that the world he lives in is quite well organised; it is divided into town (society) and all the rest that exists outside it, and the rural area too is divided into regions which have borders. Molloy often confuses these territory limits but, nevertheless, he is aware of their existence.

Moran goes even further. Before his trip to Ballybaba, he literally dwells in and for institutions, and he is respectful of common rules. He lives in a small house with a little garden and has a servant that cooks and cleans his home, he works during the week and rests at the weekend like all normal people do, he attends church, he loves punctuality and "even more, decorum" (94), he has a son that he tries to educate in a strict way, he has "a methodical mind" (90). But there are plenty of other examples. Moran works as a sort of secret agent in order to preserve institutions, he claims that "if there is one thing I abhor, it is someone coming into my room, without knocking." (94) He is well integrated in a community and he applies all the social rules or, at least, he wants to give the impression he does. In fact he affirms "I don't like men and I don't like animals. As for God he's beginning to disgust me" (97). And before leaving his house he claims "I had the joyful vision of myself far from home, from the familiar faces, from all my sheet-anchors" (115). Moran, and this is soon quite clear to the reader, hides his disgust for all aspects of social life by means of an extremely conventional behaviour; he accepts and at the same time abhors these aspects of social life. "I have no insuperable objection to a neighbour's dropping in, on a Sunday, to pay his respects, if he feels the need, though I much prefer to see nobody." (85-6) Moran acts and lives in a well defined (although stereotyped) world, and when he sets out for Ballybaba he is sure he will accomplish the task of finding Molloy, and will then come back to his well-organised world. But when he comes back he finds only destruction; his bees and hens are dead, his house is empty and cold. He restarts all his relationships (with Father Ambrose, with Hanna, with his son), but he is not able to carry them on anymore.

In order to see whether Molloy's and Moran's acts can be ordered by means of Vico's "filosofia", or to see how Beckett has applied Vico's theory, we shall come back to them after having considered some of its concepts.

We have seen how philology and philosophy have to interact in order to create a science out of history. Philology describes the facts, philosophy provides the theory. But which are the axioms of Vico's philosophy? The Neapolitan knows that history is not considered a science because it lacks those principles that could promote it to a scientific rank. Vico, influenced by a Descartian mathematical mentality, felt the necessity to produce some of these principles, calling them "degnità".

The first of Vico's beliefs to be explained is the meaning of "storia ideal eterna", or ideal project. Vico's first observation is that human history comprehends a certain kind of civil order.

> L'ordine delle cose umane procedette: che prima furono le selve, dopo i tuguri, quindi i villaggi, appresso le città, finalmente l'accademie. [...] Gli uomini prima sentono il necessario, di poi badano all'utile, appresso avvertiscono il comodo, più innanzi si dilettano del piacere, quindi si dissolvono nel lusso, e finalmente impazzano in istrappazzar [dissipare] le sostanze. [...] La

natura de' popoli prima è cruda, dipoi severa, quindi benigna, appresso dilicata, finalmente dissoluta. (204-5)

In the building of villages, towns, cities and in primitive institutions (i.e. marriage, religion, burial), Vico sees the movement of mankind towards an order which is not produced by casualty. Human beings have had the choice of using their forces in a good or in a bad manner, in the right or in the wrong way. Why did these forces turn into order? It is not possible to explain the direction taken if not by recognising in these forces something that transcends them (but, at the same time, operates in- and through them).

> La legislazione considera l'uomo qual è, per farne buoni usi nell'umana società: come della ferocia, dell'avarizia, dell'ambizione, che sono gli tre vizi che portano a travverso tutto il genere umano, ne fa la milizia, la mercatanzia e la corte, e sì la fortezza, l'opulenza e la sapienza delle repubbliche; e di questi tre grandi vizi, i quali certamente distruggerebbero l'umana generazione sopra la terra, ne fa la civile felicità. Questa degnità pruova esservi provvedenza divina e che ella sia una divina mente legislatrice, la quale delle passioni degli uomini, tutti attenuti alle loro private utilità, per le quali vivrebbero da fiere bestie dentro le solitudini, ne ha fatto gli ordini civili per gli quali vivano in una umana società. [...] Le cose fuori del loro stato naturale né vi si adagiano né vi durano. [...] Questa medesima degnità, [...] pruova che l'uomo abbia libero arbitrio, però debole, di fare delle passioni virtù; ma che da Dio è aiutato naturalmente con la divina provvidenza, e soprannaturalmente dalla divina grazia. (176-7)

Human beings have acted according to justice, limiting their passions, and holding back all other instincts. Vico affirms that humans have in built ideals of justice, beauty, truth, and that they transform their bad habits into virtues. History shows how difficult it has been to realise these ideals of justice, beauty, truth. Notwithstanding this humans have acted in order to accomplish that task and this is Vico's "idea eterna". As already seen, nothing lasts if it is not an expression of fundamental aspects of human beings.[45] Thus, what we know about the past discloses some parts of the "idea eterna", and it is in this way that the historian has to consider history. History is not due to chance or to fate. Chance does not explain the order that, slowly but continuously, has imposed itself on the world, and fate does not explain the freedom of humans to choose good or evil.

At the beginning of the trilogy, Beckett applies Vico's idea of evolution. Molloy, with his instinct is the one that "sente il necessario", and his nature is "cruda"; Moran applying his rationality "bada all'utile" and his nature can be defined "severa". It is from here on that Beckett detaches himself from Vico. Malone and the unnamable do not appreciate "il comodo", nor "si dilettano del piacere" or "si dissolvono nel lusso", and their nature is not "benigna e dilicata" nor "dissoluta". As already seen in the previous sub-chapter, it is in *Molloy* that Beckett has considered Vico's ideas; from Malone onwards, Beckett goes his own way. He too suggests a sort of development and a possible defeat, but the difference is that Beckett does not submit to Vico's "provvedenza divina", he does not want to listen to that product of a "divina mente legislatrice, la quale delle passioni degli uomini, tutti attenuti alle loro private utilità, per le quali vivrebbero da fiere bestie dentro le solitudini, ne ha fatto gli ordini civili per gli quali vivano in una umana società." (177) And, in fact, he does not, or - better said - he does not want to. But, in fact, Malone and the unnamable (and Moran too, at the end of his report) have to cope with that force. (cf. Part III, Ch. 1. on the trilogy).

Part II – "The Nothing with which to express and the Nothing from which to express"

Another fundamental principle in Vico's theory is that of the way in which a relevant social phenomenon is known. "Natura di cose altro non è che nascimento di esse in certi tempi e con certe guise, le quali sempre che sono tali, indi tali e non altre nascon le cose." (180) To understand an historical fact it is necessary to investigate its genesis, its development, and thus the conditions out of which it has developed, the modifications it has produced on the social system it has affected and on the humans that have produced it. Vico, in other words, affirms here the historical-social nature of human beings; they produce facts which influence both the social environment and people themselves. To understand the origin of a relevant social act means to be able to describe the circumstances which have produced it and its influence on the social setting and on the human race.

If we consider Molloy as the one who produces relevant social acts and Moran as a man who personifies the social system in which Molloy's acts take place, we notice that we know the circumstances that push Molloy to his rambling (the need to see his mother), but this is the only general guideline for our understanding of Molloy. All other actions, decisions, facts which involve the presence of Molloy are either due to chance or are caused by other people who interfere in Molloy's random movement. Beckett seems to suggest that casualty not only exists, but it also has a very important part in what happens to human beings. Beckett here detaches himself from Vico, and he does it in the direction which is most familiar to him i.e. that of doubt and of a conscient refusal to accept any superior authority whatsoever.

If we come back to the comparison between Vico's idea that a social act becomes relevant if it is possible to describe its influence on the social setting and on the human race, we can notice that Beckett and Vico join again. Both the social system in which Molloy lives, and Moran and Molloy themselves, are affected by Molloy's actions: because of Molloy's vicinity, Moran loses his capability to move freely and becomes aware of a voice speaking in his interiority; when

Moran comes back to his home everything has changed and his social surroundings have been destroyed. Molloy himself goes on rambling and this causes his inability to talk to his mother in order to settle the matter between them. This theoretical and empirical way warns the reader not to attribute false potentialities to humans, but to underline those historical properties which have spread out of systems and activities which have left visible signs.

> Le proprietà inseparabili da' subbietti [languages and institutions] devon essere prodotte dalla modificazione o guisa con che le cose son nate; per lo che esse ci posson avverare tale e non altra essere la natura o nascimento di esse cose. (180)

The characteristics of the subjects of history have not to be set *a priori*, but have to be the consequence of their products; it is necessary to see the modifications produced, and interpretate them bearing in mind the relationship between humans and institutions. Thus if Vico's ideal project on the one hand saves the human race from its disappearance in empiricism or in the disorder of unconnected events, on the other hand it does not allow us to concentrate on abstract theories only, but forces us to focus on the modalities of its realisation.

It is here that Beckett exasperates Vico's ideas. In the beginning, his characters act according to Vico's theory and they operate within a social and cultural frame (even Molloy obeys common rules and recognises authorities e.g. that of the policeman). But soon they lose control of what is happening and their actions become a series of unconnected events. This decay, which is the exact contrary of Vico's building up, is even more dramatic than the Neapolitan's "dissolversi nel lusso" (205) because it is not due to greed or luxury, but is the product of a rationality which does not see there is any other way to follow. An example is Moran who, victim of the failing of his theories

Part II – "The Nothing with which to express and the Nothing from which to express"

about society, is disillusioned and emarginates himself. Beckett seems to be aware and to appreciate Vico's theory, but when he tries to apply it, he is beaten by the factual confusion that rules his characters and the world. Molloy's, Moran's, Malone's and the unnamable's defeat are examples of a decay which seems to be a total refusal of the constructive alternatives offered by society.

To summarise. The theoretical setting that philosophy elaborates and offers to philology is composed of three parts.
1. The "idea eterna" or ideal project, which spreads out of those ideals of justice, truth, and beauty described by Plato. Beckett applies it only in the first part of his trilogy; Molloy and Moran interpret the two first stages of Vico's historic development in a mechanical way by applying instinct (Molloy) and order (Moran).
2. The incidence of those ideals listed in 1. on the human mind. This is the result empirical research has to attain, otherwise it would not be possible to explain the repetition of certain events in the course of history. We have seen how Beckett concentrates on Molloy's disorder overwhelming Moran's stereotyped conventions, and how the result attained by Beckett detaches itself from what is suggested by Vico. On the one hand there is the order of a divine project, on the other hand the confusion of chaos and casualty and the conscient refusal of that divine voice which leads to order.
3. To understand a historical event, it is necessary to rebuild its genesis and conditions, and its incidence on human beings. We have seen that here Beckett detaches himself from Vico (in that he does not accept the presence of a divine order) and we have then considered Molloy's deleterious influence on the social order represented by Moran.

If philosophy is, for Vico, "la scienza del vero" i.e. the science of truth, philology is "la coscienza del certo" i.e. being aware of something certain. But what is, for Vico, certainty? A first hint, as already seen, is given in his ninth "degnità". "Gli uomini che non sanno il vero delle cose proccurano d'attenersi al certo, perché, non potendo soddisfare l'intelletto con la scienza, almeno la volontà riposi sulla coscienza." (177-8) Those people that do not know the truth of things, have to conform to what is certain; not being able to satisfy their minds by means of science, they can, at least, "riposar la volontà sulla coscienza".[46] Philology is used to interpret that period of history in which humans, not being able to understand the causes and aims of certain phenomena, were satisfied by simply being aware of their existence. Philology concentrates on that long period of time when science was not yet the fundamental principle of action, and human beings were not aware of the nature of things and of the direction their actions aimed at. Molloy is a perfect example of that way of carrying through actions; he often claims that he speaks, does things and thinks, without knowing why nor what he is doing; he simply follows his instinct and a "murmur, something gone wrong with the silence" (81).[47]

Philology is concerned with language. Vico affirms: "[i] parlari volgari debbon esser i testimoni più gravi degli antichi costumi de' popoli, che si celebrarono nel tempo ch'essi si formaron le lingue." (181) These "parlari volgari" are the linguistic ways of expression on which the philologist has to concentrate: they have appeared at the same time as primitive customs and thus express their characteristics and essence. Vico underlines the extreme importance of a linguistic analysis: "[l]ingua di nazione antica, che si è conservata regnante finché pervenne al suo compimento, dev'essere un gran testimone de' costumi de' primi tempi del mondo." (181) Going further in his analyses, Vico claims that all languages stem out of a "lingua mental comune a tutte le nazioni" (185). Language, life and necessities are thus similar in all human beings irrespective of culture and geographical provenance.[48]

Philology is a science that ascertains historical facts in order to show their "sapienza volgare". It is thus not a collection of different ways in which words and grammar have changed, but the rebuilding, by means of language, of the realm of needs, passions and ideals of human beings. In this sense, Beckett's refusal of language, his showing that language fails to describe what he feels to be important, might be understood as a rejection of this common background described by Vico. Molloy's murmur, Moran's voice, Malone's occasional "here", and the unnamable's "here" and "they" are examples of Beckett's interpretation of Vico's common source of language; they appear in the characters' minds and provoke the impossibility of being silent (cf. Part III, on the trilogy). Beckett develops Vico's "lingua mental commune" into a curse that haunts his characters and that obliges them to speak.

The Three Ages of Human Society: "L'Età degli Dei", "L'Età degli Eroi", "L'Età degli Uomini"

Samuel Beckett in "Dante...Bruno.Vico..Joyce", condenses as follows Vico's thesis of the division of human society into three ages.

> In the beginning was thunder: the thunder set free Religion, in its most objective and unphilosophical form - idolatrous animism: Religion produced Society, and the first social men were the cave-dwellers, taking refuge from a passionate Nature: this primitive family life receives its first impulse towards development from the arrival of terrified vagabonds: admitted, they are the first slaves: growing stronger, they exact agrarian concessions, and a despotism has evolved into a primitive feudalism: the cave becomes a city, and the feudal system a democracy: then an anarchy: this is corrected by a return to monarchy: the last stage is a tendency

towards interdestruction: the nations are dispersed, and the Phoenix of Society arises out of their ashes (20-1)

Vico himself in his "degnità liii" claims: "[g]li uomini prima sentono senz'avvertire, dappoi avvertiscono con animo perturbato e commosso, finalmente riflettono con mente pura." (199) In Beckett's trilogy we are presented with a development which, as usual, follows in part the one described by Vico, but detaches itself from the final aims and, in part, from its structure too. Let us consider in more detail these aspects.

According to Vico the first age of human society is "l'età degli dei" or theocratic age. It is characterised by the dominance of senses and by the absence of cogitation. As already quoted, primitives "sentono senza avvertire"; an object produces an effect (agreeable, of fear, annoying) on the ancestors of humanity, and this is the reason why they notice it, otherwise the object does not exist. In Molloy's words we find Beckett's interpretation of Vico's theocratic age.

> The words engraved themselves for ever on my memory, perhaps because I understood them at once, a thing I didn't often do. Not that I was hard of hearing, for I had quite a sensitive ear, and sounds unencumbered with precise meaning were registered perhaps better by me than by most. What was it then? A defeat of the understanding perhaps, which only began to vibrate on repeated solicitations, or which did vibrate, if you like, but at a lower frequency, or a higher, than that of ratiocination, if such a thing is conceivable, and such a thing is conceivable since I conceive it. [...] I preferred the garden to the house, to judge to the long hours I spent there. (*Molloy*, 47-9)

Part II – "The Nothing with which to express and the Nothing from which to express"

Molloy hears words but he does not understand them, and he is not able to connect them with objects, facts or concepts. He supposes he likes things because he is aware of doing them; He feels like his ancestors, that things exist because they happen. But what makes Molloy different from Vico's primitives is the fact that Molloy thinks and is aware of his (non-)choices. Molloy ignores the effects produced by an action or a fact.

> But recalling who I was I soon threw away my crutch and came to a standstill in the middle of the room, determined to stop asking for things, to stop pretending to be angry. For to want my clothes, and I thought I wanted them, was no reason for pretending to be angry, when they were refused. (41)

A fact happens, Molloy perceives its existence, he has a reaction, but then he decides to ignore his reaction and the fact itself; Beckett, as already stated, exasperates Vico's ideas in that he applies them to Molloy who is not, historically speaking, a primitive, and thus is aware of what is happening and has to measure himself with the society that surrounds him.

Vico's first age is the age of total subjectivity, when something interests only if it produces an effect. Vico calls this period of time *theocratic* in that all natural phenomena were thought to be the product of a deity. Here we are back to Beckett's "[i]n the beginning was the thunder": primitives, who used signs to express themselves, interpret all natural phenomena as messages of scaring and punishing deities.[49] Which is Beckett's punishing deity that causes phenomena to happen and which is used to explain them? Molloy and Moran (when in Ballybaba) suggest a sort of murmur or voice that is not clear and thus causes things to happen without their understanding them. Molloy and Moran have to obey the voice, but their incomprehension of it causes them to be in a vicious circle. They do not understand what happens, a deity appears and tells them something, they fail to understand the deity's clarification, or if they understand it, it is only for a brief time, and thus come back to the first point, that of their incomprehension of reality. And the deity's punishment is his or her bare existence, that causes Molloy's, Moran's, Malone's, the unnamable's and Beckett's need for expression. It is an interesting development of Vico's ideas that Beckett suggests: his characters are not really part of the theocratic age (they seem to live in contemporary Ireland), but they are in some way forced to go back to that period. It is a sort of tragic regression in that Beckett's characters refuse what has been produced by history, but are not able to leave out what culture has produced.

As a consequence of "poetic theology" (as Vico calls this period when deities governed the world) the first human rulers (i.e. fathers) based their power on religion. What is important here is that poetic theology makes a whole out of itself through theocratic government and divine right. It is a sociological and metaphysical unit of the same historical period. The nature of primitives is reflected by their religious *credo*, the creed is reflected in the social organisation which is beginning to exist, and the social structure, by starting to set rules affects the primitives.

Moran is a father and one of the first times he introduces his son, it is in a religious (although standardised) contest. "I called Jacques. Without result. I said, Seeing me still in conference he has gone to mass alone. This explanation turned out subsequently to be the correct one." (87) Moran's religious *credo* is extremely conventional and constrained; he experiences it as a series of orders to be obeyed, and he tolerates them without really accepting them, because the divine does not operate in the way he wishes. "I asked the Lord for guidance. Without result." (92).[50] Moran's son is totally subject to his father; he is afraid of him and he does not react to his father's decisions, even if he does not find them right.[51] Moran bases his power over his son on a series of dogma, and he wants them to be respected as he respects institutional religious rules. His religious creed is utilitarian and in that way he manages his relationship with his son; Moran gives orders in order to control Jacques. Beckett seems to be applying Vico's ideas, he seems to appreciate the bases these concepts set, but he does not accept their development and thus parodies them (especially with Moran), and then considers them in a personal way. Vico underlines the difficulty of correctly understanding our ancestors:

> ora ci è naturalmente niegato di poter entrare nella vasta immaginativa di que' primi uomini, le menti de' quali di nulla erano astratte, di nulla erano assottigliate, di nulla spiritualizzate, perch'erano tutte immerse ne' sensi, tutte rintuzzate dalle passioni, tutte seppellite ne' corpi: onde [...] or appena intender si può, affatto immaginar non si può, come pensassero i primi uomini che fondarono l'umanità gentilesca. (265)

It is a correct description of Molloy, and of Moran's difficulty in understanding him. Vico claims that it is impossible to enter into these primitives' minds because they were full of instinct and without any rational or spiritual counterpart. As we have already seen, Molloy is in part different because he lives in a social contest, but his essence is similar to that of "que' primi uomini": Moran's losing his head and his loss of mobility when thinking of Molloy, incarnates Vico's impossibility to understand those primitives minds.

Vico's second age, "l'età degli eroi" (heroic age), is characterised by the dominance of imagination over rational thinking. The setting is described by Beckett in his "Dante...Bruno.Vico..Joyce". "[T]he first social men were the cave-dwellers, taking refuge from a passionate Nature: this primitive family life receives its first impulse towards development from the arrival of terrified vagabonds: admitted, they are the first slaves" (20). These societies were confronted with two forces; an internal and an external one. The internal is caused by social differences and is controlled by religion; "quella che regola tutto il giusto degli uomini è la giustizia divina, la quale ci è ministrata dalla divina provvedenza per conservare l'umana società." (241) As already seen, Moran incarnates Beckett's idea of society and the Irish writer uses him to show an example of control over a subordinate (Moran's son) by means of religion.

The entire destructive potential of primitive tribes can only be realised outside its structure. The external force causes thus the naissance of the heroic world, pervaded by masculine and aggressive ideals. Physical strength, blood, righteousness in combat, ferocity are all elements praised in this age. Beckett interprets this outburst of destructive power in *Malone Dies*. Malone lives in a room (a sort of cave) and, while waiting for death, tells himself stories. Imagination takes the place of reality; the setting is the same as Vico's, but, as usual, the aim is different. Vico's imagination creates heroes, Malone's rationality revolts against the fear of ultimate silence and speaks about characters which, in one way or in another, can be considered (anti-)heroes. Malone's external force is that of the characters he creates in his stories: Sapo-Macmann, the Lamberts, and Lemuel, perform those actions Malone is not able to do anymore. Malone's stories are full of violence and blood. Big Lambert "[is] highly thought of as a bleeder and disjointer of pigs" (183); he loves to kill animals (183-4); there is a careful description of his burying a mule "banging [the mule's forelegs] down with a spade" because they "projected above the level of the ground" (194). Beckett transforms Vico's Hercules who kills the lion and slays and captures other terrible beasts, into a man who loves to kill animals for no particular reason. Hercules' respect for the lion (he wears its skin) becomes Big Lambert's banging the mule's forelegs down with a spade while Hercules' heroic acts of protecting Greek people by annihilating frightening problems is transformed into Big Lambert's job as a bleeder and disjointer of pigs. Incest is not a problem for Big Lambert, and he would have "gladly slept with his daughter" (198); this is in contradiction with all the merciful and brave laws of the heroic world which describe how fathers have to vigilate and protect their children and families, how they have to be righteous. Lemuel kills Lady Pedal and her friends with a hatchet (260) destroying another law of the heroic world: that of coherence and righteousness, both in combat and in life. These examples show Beckett's interpretation of Vico's heroic world; the metaphysics which is born out of imagination is cruel: instinct takes the place of righteousness in combat, the act of killing is unexplained and has no actual justification.

The third and last age of Vico's subdivisions of history, "l'età degli uomini", or the human age, has, as its main characteristic, the advent of rationality. From a metaphysics born out of imagination (in the heroic age), history enters the realm of logic, of philosophy, of a developed metaphysics. The ideals of righteousness and truth, of which the humans of the heroic age had an intuition, become the subject of philosophical studies. It is the age of theorizing, of becoming conscious of mechanisms and thematics. The unnamable is Beckett's negative interpretation of Vico's human age. The unnamable represents the ultimate stadium of what can be achieved, although this is an unresolvable impasse. Neither rationality nor instinct, nor stories seem to be able to give an exhaustive answer to the unnamable's questions. We are already beyond Vico's faith in rationality and its being led by a divine design. The unnamable's monologue is mainly concerned with mechanisms and with theories.

To summarise. We have seen how Vico's subdivision of history into three ages is followed by Beckett in his series of novels. Vico's first age, the theocratic one, where all phenomena were produced by gods, has been outlined in *Molloy*. Molloy hears a murmur (Moran a voice) which is the mainspring of his looking for his mother (Moran looking for Molloy).

In Vico's second age, the heroic one, the power accumulated in primitive societies, creates heroes. We have seen how, in a similar way, Malone's rationality looks for an escape from its becoming silent by creating stories full of blood and violence.

Vico's third age, called the human age, is based on rationality and on the attempt to understand divine order. The unnamable is the ultimate result of Beckett's history of evolution, and he too concentrates on mechanisms and thematics, but his unattainable aim is that of being able to let his rationality become silent.

Poetry, Language, Myth

Giambattista Vico has treated other subjects that are interesting in our understanding of Beckett's writings, namely the discussion of the birth and development of language, poetry and myth. It is worth following Beckett's "Dante...Bruno.Vico..Joyce" with its "painful exposition of Vico's dynamic treatment" (26) of them.
Beckett starts by considering poetry.

> Vico rejected the three popular interpretations of the poetic spirit, which consider poetry as either an ingenious popular expression of philosophical conceptions, or an amusing social diversion, or an exact science within the research of everyone in possession of the recipe. Poetry, he says, was born of curiosity, daughter of ignorance. The first men had to create matter by the force of their imagination, and 'poet' means 'creator'. Poetry was the first operation of the human mind, and without it thought could not exist. Barbarians, incapable of analysis and abstraction, must use their fantasy to

explain what their reasons cannot comprehend. Before articulation comes song; before abstract terms, metaphors. The figurative character of the oldest poetry must be regarded, not as sophisticated confectionery, but as evidence of a poverty-stricken vocabulary and of a disability to achieve abstraction. Poetry is essentially the antithesis of Metaphysics: Metaphysics purge the mind of the senses and cultivate the disembodiment of the spiritual; Poetry is all passion and feeling and animates the inanimate; Metaphysics are most perfect when most concerned with universals; Poetry, when most concerned with particulars. Poets are the sense, philosophers the intelligence of humanity. Considering the Scholastics' axiom *'niente è nell'intelletto che prima non sia nel senso'*, it follows that poetry is a primitive condition of philosophy and civilization. The primitive animistic movement was a manifestation of the 'forma poetica dello spirito'. (23-4)

Beckett's writings are not born of curiosity, they deal with particulars and ignorance, but from a metaphysical point of view, and this is the reason for Beckett's not being able to go silent. Beckett claims that the mind of barbarians "must use their fantasy to explain what their reasons cannot comprehend". The Irish writer has developed this thought for himself; what pushes him to write is not mere fantasy which substitutes for a deficient rationality, but chaos and a refusal to submit to this need to express himself.

We become aware of the direction Beckett is taking; he wants to go back to that "poverty-stricken vocabulary", to that "disability to achieve abstraction" of the oldest poetry. It is a sort of regression to song and metaphor by means and in contrast to articulation and abstract terms, an attempt to unify Metaphysics and Poetry in that the forces he has to cope with (cf. Part I, Ch. 2. on Plato) generates the particulars of the actual stories he tells.

Beckett's movement is animistic in that it is subject to the force of objects. Molloy, for example, can be considered an animistic character; his experiences and his rambling, are examples of a collection of experiences made without understanding them. Molloy often claims that he does not know what he is doing nor why he is doing it, but he does it anyway: he is not able to abstract theories from the facts he experiences, he just passes through them, and he is not even sure of the reality of the things he describes as having happened. He is the sense and instinct of the trilogy, his vocabulary is small, but not because a vocabulary does not exist, but because he is losing it as time goes on.

Beckett carries on his analyses discussing the role of language.

> [Vico's] treatment of the origin of language proceeds along similar lines. Here again he rejected the materialistic and trascendental views; the one declaring that language was nothing but a polite and conventional symbolism; the other, in desperation, describing it as a gift from the Gods. As before, Vico is the rationalist, aware of the natural and inevitable growth of language. In its first dumb form, language was gesture. If a man wanted to say 'sea', he pointed to the sea. With the spread of animism this gesture was replaced by the word: 'Neptune'. He directs our attention to the fact that every need of life, natural, moral and economic, has its verbal expression in one or other of the 30,000 Greek divinities. This is Homer's 'language of the Gods'. Its evolution through poetry to a highly civilised vehicle, rich in abstract and technical terms, was as little fortuitous as the evolution of society itself. Words have their progressions as well as social phases. 'Forest-cabin-village-city-

academy' is one rough progression. Another: 'mountain-plain-riverbank'. And every word expands with psychological inevitability. Take the latin word 'Lex'.
1. Lex=Crop of acorns.
2. Ilex=Tree that produces acorns.
3. Legere=To gather.
4. Aquilex=He that gathers the waters.
5. Lex=Gathering together of peoples, public assembly.
6. Lex=Law.
7. Legere=To gather together letters into a word, to read.

The root of any word whatsoever can be traced back to some prelingual symbol. This early inability to abstract the general from the particular produced the Type-names. It is the child's mind over again. The child extends the names of the first familiar objects to other strange objects in which he is conscious of some analogy. The first men, unable to conceive the abstract idea of 'poet' or 'hero', named every hero after the first hero, every poet after the first poet. Recognizing this custom of designating a number of individuals by the names of their prototypes, we can explain various classical and mythological mysteries. Hermes is the prototype of the Egyptian inventor: so for Romulus, the great law-giver, and Hercules, the Greek hero: so for Homer. Thus Vico asserts the spontaneity of language and denies the dualism of poetry and language. Similarly, poetry is the foundation of writing. When language consisted of gesture, the spoken and written were identical. Hieroglyphics, or sacred language, as he calls it, were not the invention of philosophers for the mysterious expression of profound thought, but the common necessity of primitive peoples. Convenience only begins to assert itself at a far more advanced stage of civilization, in the form of alphabetism. Here Vico, implicitly at least, distinguishes between writing and direct expression. In such direct expression, form and content are inseparable. Examples are the medals of the Middle Ages, which bore no inscription and were a mute testimony to the feebleness of conventional alphabetic writing: and the flags of our own day. (24-5)

Beckett tries to go back to the prelingual symbol which is the root of any word: he does it in a destructive way; he denies all abstract meaning but uses the words anyway because there is no other means of communication that can communicate the inability to communicate. Thus, in his trilogy, words have been created in order to describe seen objects and concepts correlated with these objects (it is an attempt to go back to "the child's mind"), but they have become so detached from what they should describe that they have lost all relation with it. Molloy, Moran, Malone and the unnamable speak, but the words they use are only a conventional means used to express conventional meanings. Beckett revolts against that language in that he makes it fail his characters and in that he lets them claim that what they have said, say and will be saying is nothing but meanless sounds with no relation to the truth of silence. The unnamable's quest for peace through silence is a rejection of something useless, but his final "I will go on" (382) shows how, for Beckett, it is impossible to find a new means of expression.

But what is important here is the fact that Beckett's language, in the trilogy, is trying go get back to Vico's "mute testimony". The unnamable's silence and immobility should be a hieroglyphic which directly refers to the conclusion it wants to describe, and makes it possible to transform him into the prototype of the characters of the trilogy, a sort of living (if he is actually *living*) *Ursprache* that interprets the common necessities of contemporary-primitive people. For Beckett there are no first heroes nor first poets he can refer to, and thus he refers directly to the essence of those things he is concerned with; he does not consider objects but only ideas of objects. Beckett is looking for an *Ursprache* that has no relation anymore with the world of objects.

Beckett finally considers myth.

> As with Poetry and Language, so with Myth. Myth, according to Vico, is neither an allegorical expression of general philosophical axioms (Conti, Bacon), nor a derivative from particular peoples, as for instance the Hebrews or Egyptians, nor yet the work of isolated poets, but an historical statement of fact, of actual contemporary phenomena, actual in the sense that they were created out of necessity by primitive minds, and firmly believed. Allegory implies a threefold intellectual operation: the construction of a message of general significance, the preparation of a fabulous form, and an exercise of considerable technical difficulty in uniting the two, an operation totally beyond the reach of the primitive mind. Moreover, if we consider the myth as being essentially allegorical, we are not obliged to accept the form in which it is cast as a statement of fact. But we know that the actual creators of these myths gave full credence to their face-value. Jove was no symbol: he was terribly real. It was precisely their superficial metaphorical character that made them intelligible to people incapable of receiving anything more abstract than the plain record of objectivity. (25-6)

Beckett's explanation of Vico's view of myth is extremely important for our understanding of the work of the Irish writer. Beckett claims that myth is not an allegory of philosophical ideas but a real fact, in that it embodies the necessity of primitives to understand those phenomena they were confronted with. Beckett's works are similar in that they give voice to a necessity. Again, the difference between Vico and Beckett is in the kind of mind which has that necessity; Vico considers primitive minds, Beckett is concerned with his - modern - mind, which denies its rationality in order to get back to that silence which existed even before the birth of myth. "Jove was no symbol", neither are Vladimir, Estragon nor Godot; they interpret a force that objectively exists, but which cannot become abstract because it is outside rational reach (cf. Part I, Ch. 3. on mysticism).[52] The mistake Vico stigmatises in historians is the same that Moran does when considering Molloy. Moran thinks of Molloy as a number, as one of the missions he has to accomplish. But he will be ruined by this belief; like Jove, so "terribly real", Molloy changes Moran's life although the two do not even meet. Primitives were incapable of receiving anything more abstract than the plain record of objectivity, Moran is incapable of challenging his rational and objective view of the world and thus needs a Jove to terrify him.

The unnamable often speaks of myths that "they" have tried and still try to stuff into his mind e.g. after having told the story of the woman that marries twice, he claims "it is the return to the world of fable, no, just a reminder, to make me regret what I have lost, long to be again in the place I was banished from, unfortunately it doesn't remind me of anything." (375) We notice how Beckett destroys Vico's reality of facts described in myths, and how he lets them become an abstraction of a mind which has no more necessities. The unnamable's conclusive myth is that of the existence of "there", of a place where life goes on, and which he has refused to recognise. The mythological figures are all the characters that have preceded the unnamable, Mercier and Camier, Watt, Molloy, Moran, Malone, Mahood and Worm. They incarnate the unnamable in the world of "there", and, as we can read their stories in Beckett's novels, they are

Part II – "The Nothing with which to express and the Nothing from which to express"

not symbols but real characters, perfect objective descriptions of a certain aspect of reality. But, in the unnamable's words, they are unreal, they do not exist, they are merely an attempt of "them" to let the unnamable believe the real existence of "there".

The unnamable, the last character and thus the "historian" of the trilogy, reconsiders and gives a structure to what has happened before he appeared. The result is double: on the one hand we are given a key for the lecture of the preceding parts (although it seems to be a very complex one), on the other we are not, in Beckett words, "obliged to accept the form in which [these stories are] cast as a statement of fact." (26)

Human Beings and History

The role of humans in history is extremely clear for Vico:

> in tal densa notte di tenebre ond'è coverta la prima da noi lontanissima antichità, apparisce questo lume eterno, che non tramonta, di questa verità, la quale non si può a patto alcuno chiamar in dubbio: che questo mondo civile egli certamente è stato fatto dagli uomini, onde se ne possono, perché se ne debbono, ritruovare i princìpi dentro le modificazioni della nostra medesima mente umana. (231-2)

Humanity is the protagonist of history. In the chapter about "Filosofia" and "Filologia" we have seen that history retroactively has an effect on men and women, but what are the results of this influence? The first and most important one is that human beings are attracted by socialisation, and this in spite of the fact that by doing so they lose part of their freedom and have to temperate their passions. We have an example of that mechanism in Moran's life; he is attracted by and lives in society but, in doing so, he has to accept certain rules and this causes his refusal of many aspects of associate living. The modification that society undergoes can be explained with the change of the human mind, Vico claims; the mind of Beckett's characters is becoming more and more confused and empty, and society slowly disappears from the trilogy's world.

A second result of the influence of history on people is that humanity has the freedom of choice: "[l]'umano arbitrio, di sua natura incertissimo, egli si accerta e determina col senso comune degli uomini d'intorno alle umane necessità o utilità, che son i due fonti del diritto natural delle genti." (178) History is not the product of a cosmic need or of casualty; both these views cannot explain the actual course of history. History is what humans wanted it to be, with the inevitable limitations due to conditions and means at their disposal. "L'uman arbitrio", free-will, is always uncertain; it is only by causing a result that it becomes plain and evident. Molloy represents free-will; his rambling across Ballyba and his confusion are dangers society has to cope with. In fact, Moran will be defeated by Molloy's force and Moran will not be the same again after his coming back home. Beckett's free-will causes confusion and doubt, and the society he sketches is going in that direction.

But how is free-will conciliable with the following passage, which we find on page 705 of Vico's *Scienza Nuova*?

> Perché pur gli uomini hanno essi fatto questo mondo di nazioni [...] ma egli è questo mondo, senza dubbio, uscito da una mente spesso diversa ed alle volte tutta contraria e sempre superiore ad essi fini particolari ch'essi uomini si avevan proposti; quali lini ristretti, fatti mezzi per servire a fini più ampi, gli ha sempre adoperati per conservare l'umana generazione in questa terra.

Vico claims the existence of a superior entity which acts uncontrolled and is not influenced by humans. The aim of this entity is to preserve "l'umana generazione in questa terra" (706). Even egoistic human decisions turn into productive results.

> Imperciocché vogliono gli uomini usar la libidine bestiale e disperdere i loro parti, e ne fanno la castità de' matrimoni, onde surgono le famiglie; vogliono i padri esercitare smoderatamente gl'imperi paterni sopra i clienti, e gli assoggetiscono agli imperi civili, onde surgono le città; vogliono gli ordini regnanti de' nobili abusare la libertà signorile sopra i plebei, e vanno in servitù delle leggi, che fanno la libertà popolare; vogliono i popoli liberi sciogliersi dal freno delle lor leggi, e vanno nella soggezion de' monarchi; vogliono i monarchi, in tutti i vizi della dissolutezza che gli assicuri, invilire i loro sudditi, e gli dispongono a sopportare la schiavitù di nazioni più forti; vogliono le nazioni disperdere se medesime, e vanno a salvare gli avanzi dentro le solitudini, donde, qual fenice, nuovamente risurgano. (706)

According to Vico, history does not evolve against or independently of human beings. History is the place where hidden and inmost thoughts of human nature become understandable and thus increase and sharpen humanity's spirit.

This superior entity, called by Vico "Divine Providence", operates in humans by means of an Ideal Project which is not a product of human beings nor a product of history. The project is never clearly understandable because it is present in men and women, but has not been created by them; it is present in history but it cannot be explained by means of it. The ideals of justice, good, truth, are realised or denied in history, but they are not at the mercy of humans nor of history. Although influenced by these ideals, humans do not master them. The ideal project is the means by which human beings are in communication with God; it is the bridge between eternity and transience, between transcendence and history. At the completion of his theory, Vico comes back to the polemics between the scientific and the humanistic view of the world. If Galileo had described God as a geometrician, Vico's God is "provvidente". The ties between divine and human are not of a mathematical kind (mathematics is a human product and cannot totally explain reality), but of an ideal kind: the union is possible only in history, where the dependence of human is clearly shown, and where the kinship between God and human beings reveals itself. It is at this point that Beckett leaves Vico, Galileo and Descartes; he cannot accept a rationalistic view of the world (but he has to cope with it), and he is not able to totally accept Vico's God and its consequent ideal project. Thus we reach the impasse which haunts us at the end of *The Unnamable*.[53]

According to Vico, history is not a linear process, free of mistakes, evil and decadence; rationality may fail, and a lazy society may fall back to barbarism and cruelty. Divine Providence is universal, but its action is not a must; humans may act according to it, but they are free to deny it. Beckett's situation is different in that he is not lazy, but consciously decides not to follow what he feels he is obliged to do, but then he is not able to resist. Even when humanity fails to understand Providence, this does not disappear but restarts again in showing the right way to humans. Would it not be so, Vico concludes, no nation would have survived and all would be condemned to disappear. Even Beckett is aware of the permanency of *something* (to call it "Divine Providence" is not appropriate in the case of Beckett) that obliges him to act in a particular way, but his refusal to submit to that voice creates a situation where disappearance is not attained, but the voice is not strong enough to show him Vico's "right way".

PART III - "THE OBLIGATION TO EXPRESS"

BECKETT AND THE SEARCH FOR A SENSE

PROSE: THE TRILOGY

In Part I and Part II I have tried to describe Beckett's *unknown*, and to establish a vocabulary which should help readers to name and try to understand the particular forces that permeate Beckett's works. Part III is the direct consequence of the preceding ones; it applies the theoretical results I have achieved to Beckett's actual writings. How does Beckett mix the various parts that make up the unknowable, in order to look for a sense? In Part III we will see that Beckett develops his research in all possible directions. He never concentrates on a single aspect only, but is always aware of the presence of the others, and fuses them into a whole that tries to be omnipresent, omniscient and omninegating. I have chosen to concentrate on *Molloy*, *Malone Dies* and *The Unnamable* because the trilogy is Beckett's longest work and it presents the amplest treatment and development of the forces we are interested in.[54] It is worth saying that I will not attempt any symbolical interpretation, such as the fact that in the trilogy the true self can rest from self caricature, or that in it Beckett gives voice to his dream of failure, or that the four characters may stand for human decay and death, and I will not debate if Moran becomes Molloy (or vice-versa), and Molloy transforms himself into Malone and in the unnamable. These are possibilities, but that kind of interpretation is left to the direct reader of the trilogy and to the particular psychological phase in which he finds himself at the moment of reading. Notice that this sort of particular interpretations are extremely deceitful because the characters of the trilogy

> appear to "associate" not with the real *or* with their audience but only with themselves. [...] Yet this self-containment is also self-explosive. For the *activity* of this narcissistic concentration is extraordinarily agitated. The work is continually finding itself in other parts of

itself - although what it finds is also always different from itself. And the difference is what saves the work from collapsing into a deathlike and ultimately chimerical immobility in which each of its parts would accurately reflect all its other parts. (Bersani, 6)

What is important is that even these possibilities exist. I will try to understand *how*, in the course of the trilogy, Beckett develops his relation with language, rationality and spirituality. Notice that the title of Part III is "Beckett and the *Search* for a Sense" and not "Beckett and the *Discovery* of a Sense". I am interested in mechanisms and the reason for these mechanisms.

To analyse the trilogy, I have divided it according to movement. The first sub-chapter deals with Molloy's rambling and Moran's journey to Ballybaba, what causes these movements, what they consist of, why they stop. The second sub-chapter is concerned with Malone's loss of mobility, the changes he has to cope with, how he presents what I have said about mobility. The last sub-chapter deals with the unnamable and his frustration, his attempt to go silent and to detach himself from any form of movement whatsoever.

Molloy's and Moran's Mobility

Movement is not so common in Beckett. Action, in his plays and novels, is usually confined to a delimited space in which the characters have little room for movement. The setting of *Waiting for Godot* is a definite piece of a country road, that of *Endgame* is a bare interior for Hamm and Clov, and two dustbins for Nagg and Nell, that of *Happy Days* is an explanade of scorched grass rising centre to a low mound, that of *Krapp's Last Tape* is Krapp's den, that of *Malone Dies* is Malone's room, and that of *The Unnamable* is a fixed place because the unnamable cannot move. In addition to these strong delimitations, there is the fact that Beckett's characters are not able or do not want to leave these places definitively. Vladimir and Estragon leave the road at night but come back the following day; Clov goes into the kitchen but is often recalled by Hamm, Nagg and Nell appear and disappear in a vertical movement, Krapp goes backstage but always reappears, attracted by the tape-recorder.

To these examples, some of which will be dealt with in the following sub-chapters, there is an exception, partly at least. It is *Molloy*, a novel which contains two stories describing two journeys, that of Molloy and that of Moran. The two parts of the novel are narrated by the two protagonists, at the end of their rambling, in a sort of flashback, and that is why *Molloy* is only partly an exception to the standstill.

Molloy and Three Kinds of Movement: Physical, Mental and Linguistic

When writing, Molloy is in his mother's room and Moran has barricaded himself in his house. Nevertheless their stories are not filtered by elapsed time and an ensuing failing memory nor by meditation on what has happened; the narration takes place shortly after the end of the journey, and is as vivid as if it were happening at the time of writing. That of Molloy and Moran is not a vague remembering, but a total recall.[55] We can consider Molloy as rambling; time cannot have brought confusion into his memory because he was completely confused before his narration and at the time of his writing. Molloy writes "[b]ut it is only since I have ceased to live that I think of these things and the other things. It is in the tranquillity of decomposition that I remember the long confused emotion which was my life, and that I judge it," but he immediately adds that "[t]o decompose is to live too, I know, I know, don't torment me, but one sometimes forgets." (25)[56] If in the first passage Molloy seems to have reached a definitive point of view which could enable him to remember and judge his life, his second sentence demonstrates both his confusion (he forgets things) and his unreliability as a narrator (he denies his reliability by negating seemingly pondered, just pronounced statements).

Molloy's movement is triple. The most obvious is the physical one and can be summarised as his journey to his mother. The second sign of mobility is Molloy's mind, which is to some extent independent of his will and of the effects of the world. An example.

> Yes, the words I heard, and heard distinctly, having quite a sensitive hear, were heard a first time, then a second, and often even a third, as pure sounds, free of all meaning, and this is probably one of the reasons why conversation was unspeakably painful to me. (47)

Molloy states that his mind does not register spoken words until a second or even a third hearing. There is a distance, between Molloy and his mind, which has to be bridged. The fulfilment of this distance, and its understanding is Molloy's second journey. The third kind of movement can be found in Molloy's use of language and is strongly tied up with the second one. As we have seen in the previous quotation, Molloy finds conversation "unspeakably painful", and not only when speaking to an interlocutor but also when speaking to himself. In his monologue, Molloy uses and misuses verbal forms, vocabulary, structures and their usage. With the aid of the contradiction that can be made with language, Molloy shows both the fragility of linguistic structures and of the world that they want to describe.

Molloy's journey begins "in the second or third week of June", as he "declare[s] without further ado" on page 17. Having woken up between eleven o'clock and midday, and having heard the angelus which has recalled him of incarnation, he decides to go and see his mother. The need to visit her is real for Molloy.

> And though there were many things I could do without thinking, not knowing what I was going to do until it was done, and not even then, going to my mother was not one of them. My feet, you see, never took me to my mother unless they received a definite order to do so. (29)

Molloy decides to see his mother in spite of the numerous other possibilities open to him. He has to think of this action and he has to order his feet to take him there. Nevertheless, he takes this decision and it is the only one that constantly accompanies him in his rambling. On certain occasions, Molloy seems to desist (when he leaves the town in which he supposes his mother lives, when he tries to commit suicide by cutting his wrist, when he is held up in Lousse's house, when he goes to the seaside or into the forest), but always, after a more or less short time, his mother's image oppresses him and he has to set out to see her again.

Molloy is anxious about his mother. "I shall try and speak calmly [about her]" (18). Who is Molloy's mother? He describes her as a blind, deaf, sexless woman with whom communication is possible only by knocking on her skull according to a simple code which she, having a poor memory, does not understand. It is thus not communication that draws Molloy towards his mother's room. On page 60 Molloy gives us a first clue as to the reason for his need to see her.

> I should soon find my mother and settle the matter between us. And even the nature of that matter grew dim, for me, without however vanishing completely. For it was no small matter and I was bent on it. All my life, I think, I had been bent on it. Yes, so far as I was capable of being bent on anything all a lifetime long, and what

a lifetime, I had been bent on settling this matter between my mother and me, but had never succeeded.

Molloy has a matter to settle between himself and his mother. He still does not explain what this matter is (he will later), but he affirms that it is important and that he has been concerned with it all his life long. Only four pages before the end of his narration Molloy explains why he is attracted to his mother and, at the same time, gives a reason for his rambling.

> And of myself, all my life, I think I had been going to my mother, with the purpose of establishing our relations on a less precarious footing. And when I was with her, and I often succeeded, I left her without having done anything. And when I was no longer with her I was again on my way to her, hoping to do better the next time. And when I appeared to give up and to busy myself with something else, or with nothing at all any more, in reality I was hatching my plans and seeking the way to her house. (80)

Molloy is concerned with problems of communication; he looks for a base on which to establish a less precarious relationship, but he does not know what this base should consist of, nor how to structure it. In despair, he leaves his mother, and when he is not with her anymore the necessity to see her again reappears. Molloy's physical journey is thus circular; in his mother's presence he tries to renew his relationship with her, fails, and leaves her. Her image then oppresses him, so he proceeds towards her house, reaches her and everything starts again. This cyclical movement could be interrupted in two ways. The first would be that Molloy finally succeeds in communicating with his mother. This would be the solution Molloy would prefer and would break the circle, allowing a new linear development of their relationship. But Molloy fails to exploit that possibility. The second possibility, which actually takes place, is that one of the two parts is not available anymore. Molloy is led into his mother's room but she is not there and he suspects that she is dead. At this point the circle is broken and Molloy does not need to ramble anymore. And in fact his account ends by suggesting that he will not move from that room. His mother is dead and he cannot move because of his great age. Thus both supports of his rambling desert him. The situation could seem tragic because Molloy's intention is definitely frustrated. The circle has been broken, but no further development seems possible.

It is at this point that the mental and linguistic journeys can be introduced. They are to be found throughout Molloy's account and they deeply influence his relationship with his mother. In Molloy's narration they are used both to justify his defeat (his inability to communicate) and to permit the continuity of the circularity of the narration. Molloy's confused story suggests that there might be innumerable variations and the one he has told is only one possibility among the others. "And I for my part will never lend myself to such a perversion (of the truth), until such time as I am compelled or find it convenient to do so." (70) Molloy will not contradict himself unless he so wishes (and we know how precarious his decisions are) or until he is forced to. Molloy's truth is the particular version he is narrating, it is not static but continuously changing. If Molloy never excludes a possibility and consequently creates a potentially endless story, it is because of these two aspects of his mobility.

A clarification, a microcosm of Molloy's mental and linguistic journey, is the story of A and C. After having set the situation (A going towards the town, C on his way towards the hills), and after their brief meeting, he describes them carefully. We shall consider, as an example, the description of the man returning to the town.

> But after all what was there particularly urban in his aspect? He was bare-headed, wore sand-shoes, smoked a cigar. He moved with a kind of loitering indolence which rightly or wrongly seemed to me expressive. But all that proved nothing, refuted nothing. Perhaps he had come from afar, from the other end of the island even, and was approaching the town for the first time or returning to it after a long absence. (13)

Molloy's description starts by being doubtful about the meaning of the word "urban". In an attempt to define that concept, he describes the man's clothes and attitudes. Then he considers that these elements could prove the urbanity of the man but could also deny it. At this moment, Molloy thinks of another possibility; maybe the man is approaching the town for the first time or after a long absence. Shortly after he questions himself on the improbability of the man having made such a long journey with that kind of clothing and returns to his first idea, the man is taking a walk outside the ramparts.

> But would he have come from afar, bare-headed, in sand-shoes, smoking a cigar, followed by a pomeranian? Did he not seem rather to have issued from the ramparts, after a good dinner, to take his dog and himself for a walk, like so many citizens, dreaming and farting, when the weather is fine? But was not perhaps in reality the cigar a cutty, and were not the sand-shoes boots, hobnailed, dust-whitened?" (13)

When everything seems clarified, Molloy asks himself if his description of the man is true, and gives another version. Molloy's description could seem, although contradictive (four "but" in 13 lines), rationally structured; he makes a supposition, tries to demonstrate it, fails, makes another supposition, confronts it with the first one, draws a conclusion, compares it with his starting point, etc. But his description is not rational; Molloy claims, in the gap between the two previous quotations, that "the less I think of it [if the man's dog is a pomeranian], the more certain I am." Molloy is not rational because he is not interested in the results of his speech; he does not try to demonstrate something he is interested in. Molloy's movement in language can be intuited in Molloy's arguing that the cigar might be a cutty and the sand-shoes boots. He is not sure that the objects he sees are actually what he describes them to be. Added to this difficulty, there is the problem of not knowing if the words he uses are correct for describing these objects. A clarifying explanation is to be found on page 81.

> And when I say I said, etc., all I mean is that I knew confusedly things were so, without knowing exactly what it was all about. And every time I say, I said this, or, I said that, or speak of a voice saying, far away inside me, Molloy, and then a fine phrase more or less clear and simple, or find myself compelled to attribute to others intelligible words, or hear my own voice uttering to others more or less articulate sounds, I am merely complying with the convention that demands you either lie or hold your peace.

Molloy does not posses the meaning of words, he does not reason with the aid of words, but by sensations only. Molloy lacks the mental structures which would enable him to translate his intuitions into words. He has to do it because otherwise he would not be understandable. But if he uses words, albeit unwillingly, he must have learned them in a previous stage of his life. In fact, Molloy on the first page of the novel says "I'd forgotten how to spell too, and half the words" (9). Molloy knows language and words, but is forgetting them; something has caused and is causing, at the moment of the

Part III – "The Obligation to express"

narration, this loss. Molloy explains it with a murmur, "something gone wrong with the silence" (81). The communication of that murmur is described by Molloy as follows.

> Or which I express without sinking to the level of oratio recta, but by means of other figures quite as deceitful, as for example, It seemed to me that, etc., or, I had the impression that, etc., for it seemed to me nothing at all, and I had no impression of any kind, but simply somewhere something had changed, so that I too had to change, or the world too had to change, in order for nothing to be changed. (81)

Every statement that seems deceitful in Molloy's account is even more complicated than the reader may have thought. Molloy tries to live in the world created by his inner voice and tries to impose it on the world outside himself. He seeks stability, he tries to be in harmony with himself, with the murmur, with the world. But he is aware that with words this harmony cannot be reached; a new way of communication must be found. "I might doubtless have expressed otherwise and better, if I had gone to the trouble. And so I shall perhaps some day when I have less horror of trouble than today." (81) Molloy admits that a better way of expression may be found but that he has failed to find it because of his horror of trouble, and suggests that he will perhaps try "some day". In the two sub-chapters about Malone and the unnamable we will analyse the development of Molloy's expression and rejection of language, but now we must dedicate some more time to them.

We will consider some peculiarities of Molloy's mind and, consequently, of his language and see if they really help Molloy in his need for a harmonic standstill.

Molloy's mind is stimulated by three different sources, an instinctive, a rational, and a spiritual one. Instinct is the lowest source; it is the one that pushes Molloy to act without taking into account what he is doing. Examples are his attempt to run away after having run over Lousse's dog (31-2), his fear of physical pain ("I am full of fear, I have gone in fear all my life, in fear of blows. Insult, abuse, these I can easily bear, but I could never get used to blows." 22), his spending some time at the seaside, feeling no worse there than anywhere else (63), his "going with the wind" (56) or "setting off towards the sun" (58). Molloy presents these actions as facts, without commenting on them. His language reports these events in the simplest way; he does not use deceitful figures like "I think" or "it seemed to me that". These are the facts of which the plot consists. Molloy's instinctive behaviour links him with the animal kingdom, in which actions are performed mechanically without wickedness, and reactions are caused by fear.

The second source that influences Molloy's mind is the rational one. It is the most obvious and the one most present throughout the novel. The rational part superimposes on the instinctive one and modifies it. On page 41, Molloy becomes angry because Lousse's valet tells him that his clothes have been sent to the dyers, but soon his rationality stops him.

> But recalling who I was I soon threw away my crutch and came to a standstill in the middle of the room, determined to stop asking for things, to stop pretending to be angry. For to want my clothes, and I thought I wanted them, was no reason for pretending to be angry, when they were refused.

Sentences like "recalling who I was", "determined to stop", "was no reason for pretending", show how Molloy's behaviour is regulated by his rationality. His language would seem even aristocratic if it were not for his "pretending to be angry". Molloy is not really angry and he is not really controlling his anger, he puts on an act. His rationality creates faked instincts (in this case anger) and false control over them. Molloy does not care either for his clothes or for his anger. It is in these cases that Molloy's rationality becomes nihilism and fails to affirm itself. Nothing has value for Molloy, nothing is sufficiently important to cause an alteration in his mind. When emotion would be the normal reaction to an event, he pretends to feel it but at the same time claims that he is not really involved. His rationality prevents him from concentrating on a particular object or event because he puts a barrier between himself and the object e.g. "For to want my clothes, and I thought I wanted them". Molloy is not sure he wants his clothes, he *thinks* he wants them.[57]

Molloy puts a filter between himself and events and is conscious of doing so. On page 42 he affirms that " [i]t was I who was not natural enough to enter into that order of things and appreciate its richness." He is aware of his unnatural behaviour being prevented by his rationality. This rationality is so powerful that it also influences Molloy's body. "And at first I did actually seem to feel a little better, but little by little I acquired the conviction that such was not the case." (57) In the beginning Molloy "feels" his condition, and then he "acquires the conviction" that what he has felt before is not true. Molloy's rationality overwhelms his instinct also at the level of physical pain. Molloy rejects these two sources; he subdues his instinct to his rationality, and he negates rationality with nihilism.

The third and last source is the spiritual one. Molloy claims that

> I could not, stay in the forest I mean, I was not free to. That is to say I could have, physically nothing could have been easier, but I was not purely physical, I lacked something, and I would have had the feeling, if I had stayed in the forest, of going against an imperative, at least I had that impression. (79)

In this passage Molloy resumes his instinct ("physically nothing could have been easier"), and his rationality ("at least I had that impression"), and he mentions his spiritual source "I would have had the feeling of going against an imperative". Molloy has to submit to an imperative; on page 57 he defines it. "There are things from time to time, in spite of everything, that impose themselves on the understanding with the force of axioms, for unknown reasons." There is a force that compels Molloy to perform some action in spite of his instinct and his rationality. In Molloy's narration this force is mentioned in connection with his need to visit his mother. "So I knew my imperatives well, and yet I submitted to them. It had become a habit. It is true they nearly all bore on the same question, that of my relations with my mother." (79-80) The spiritual force appears and haunts Molloy at regular intervals, namely whenever he has forgotten it.

> "Yes, these imperatives were quite explicit and even detailed until, having set me in motion at last, they began to falter, then went silent, leaving me there like a fool who neither knows where he is going nor why he is going there" (80)

The imperatives work like the goad in *Act Without Words II*, appearing at particular moments to spur action. The spiritual force is the most powerful of the three; it directly impresses its orders on Molloy, and he accomplishes them. He starts to, at least, because his rationality (always shifting the focus from where it is), and his instinct (with the impulsive reaction fear implies), soon make him forget the order of the imperative, leaving him "like a fool".

These three sources bring us back to Molloy's cyclical physical journey; the instinctive is overwhelmed by the rational one, which is made powerless by the spiritual one, which is overwhelmed by the instinctive and the rational one. Molloy is prey to that mechanism which deeply influences his mental journey. The continuous succession of the three sources causes Molloy's distance from his mind, because he is not able to identify with it. Molloy's attempt to regulate his mind deals only with the rational source. He does not try to find a harmony between the three forces, but tries to subject his instinct and spirit to the structures he makes up. He does not use rationality to make the other two sources more understandable, he tries to fit them into his reasoning. But the two other forces, with their continuous reaffirmation, inflict severe defeats upon Molloy's rationality.

Like the physical journey, the mental one can be described as a vicious circle. Again the solution would be to break the circle made up of contrasts, and develop a new relationship among the three based on a harmonic connection. Instincts and spirituality should feed rationality in order to allow its development, which would help to understand them better. But again Molloy fails and his narration stops with that problem still unresolved.

Molloy's reaction to that defeat is his use of language. Molloy is conscious of the importance and strength of language. "If I go on long enough calling that my life I'll end up by believing it. It's the principle of advertising." (50) Molloy affirms that by describing his existence as "life", he could be deceived and believe it. His linguistic mobility is, similarly to the physical and mental ones, a source of tension. Molloy wants to annihilate the force of language, so he struggles with it in order to destroy it.

To accomplish his destructive task, Molloy proceeds on two levels, an explicit and a more subtle one. The explicit level is applied when Molloy directly refers to the process of writing, or to the meaning of words and sentences. This level is mainly used by Molloy in his mother's room at the end of his rambling. It is usually a comment on the use or purpose of language. "And all the less so as whatever I do, that is to say whatever I say" (43). Molloy's words create reality but a tricky and false one. Molloy, with the help of grammatical rules, destroys the impression the reader may have had. "I speak in the present tense, when speaking of the past" (26), or "[t]here must be a touch of autumn in the air, as the saying is" (56), or "I said, if only your poor mother could see you now. I'm no enemy of the commonplace." (87) In the first two sentences, Molloy employs the "mythological present" (26) and describes an action that has taken place in the past as if it were in the present. He is conscious that the reader thinks that his sentence is reporting an actual fact, a habit Molloy has, and so he makes the reader's certainty less firm and steady by recalling that he is speaking of the past. What he is saying seems present, but is unreal. The second example is not based on language itself but shows how Molloy's statements are a mere linguistic product i.e. sounds with no connection with the real object they describe. Molloy's "as the saying is" demonstrates that he uses these words because they form the standard sentence which describes what he wants to express. His feeling is probably different, but he does not find any correlative in language.

The impossibility of describing, by means of words, what he needs to express, ends up in resignation. In the third example, Molloy affirms his indifference (even with sadistic pleasure) towards his linguistic choices, although he knows they are unacceptable. Not only does he not try to renew language, but he also makes use of commonplace. Again the reader is intentionally deceived by Molloy's language and his rational comment on it.

The agony of language in Molloy's mind ("I've forgotten how to spell too, and half the words", 9) is underlined by his rationality. An example is Molloy's speech on regions.

> For if my region had ended no further than my feet could carry me, surely I would have felt it changing slowly. For regions do not suddenly end, as far as I know, but gradually merge into one another. [...] On the other hand, if it's true that regions gradually merge

into one another, and this remains to be proved, then I will have left mine many times, thinking I was still within it. (61)

Molloy's doubt stems from a linguistic choice (he is not really interested in regions). Do regions *end* or do they *merge into one another*? In the first sentence he affirms that regions end, in the second he says that, as far as he knows, they do not end but merge into one another, while a few lines below he claims that the fact of regions merging into one another remains to be proved. His linguistic dilemma gives free play to his rationality, which underlines how little Molloy is interested in the sense of his speeches, and shows, at the same time, that his words constantly lessen their own meaning. Molloy's indecision and his usage of rationality, which underlines it, make the reader aware of a situation in which language has no clear meaning anymore. As already seen, Molloy lacks those mental structures which would enable him to translate his intuitions into words. His use of language is concerned with his rationality, which we know has a nihilistic effect.

There are a few exceptions to that mechanism which involves Molloy's nihilistic rationality and his (striving for) inexpressive language. The most surprising of them is a sentence pronounced by Molloy describing his relationship with women. "And God forgive me to tell you the horrible truth, my mother's image sometimes mingles with theirs, which is literally unendurable, like being crucified, I don't know why and I don't want to." (55) Molloy's instinct pushes him to mix his mother's image with that of his lovers, and causes great trouble in his mind, which reacts in its normal manner i.e. by refusing to analyse it ("I don't know why and I don't want to"). What is astonishing is his first reaction, which still defies rationalisation. Molloy uses a standardised sentence, "God forgive me to tell you the truth," and mingles it with an uncommon adjective for his vocabulary: "horrible". Molloy does not reject that commonplace, nor does he comment on it, making the reader aware of its presence. He is so involved (we have seen how adjectives have to be carefully considered when referring to Molloy's relationship with his mother) that his rational systematic destruction of language does not take place.

Molloy's mother, symbol of his physical journey, subdues his mental journey and his movement in language; Molloy's attempt to communicate prevails over his nihilism and his destructive way of expression. His attempt lasts only the little time needed by his rationality to regain control over it. Nevertheless, this example shows how Molloy's destructive mechanism is not perfect and how sometimes, led by his instinct, he fails to apply it.

To summarise. We have seen that Molloy's movement, although apparently chaotic, follows a circular structure. His physical journey starts and ends in his mother's presence and its goal is that of establishing a less precarious relationship. In Molloy we find many things mingled together, instinct and rationality, spirituality and irresponsibility, grotesque and genius, and this blend creates a unique character. Molloy's mental journey tries to superimpose itself on instinct and to rationalise spiritual intuitions. The third movement, that in language, aims at describing concepts (that words fail to describe) by subjecting them to a nihilistic and scientific rationality. The three movements are endlessly circular in that Molloy fails to accomplish his tasks and consequently tries again and again.[58] Existence is stronger than knowledge, in Molloy. At the time of Molloy's writing, something seems to have changed; his mother is dead, words begin to fail him, his mind slowly departs from his conscience. In other words, movement is coming to a definitive standstill. Unfortunately, with no solution in sight.

Moran

Moran's movement is based on Molloy. If he leaves his house, it is because he receives the order to see about Molloy, his body starts to ache when he decides to walk to Ballybaba, he loses his rationality when forming an opinion of Molloy. Moran exacerbates some of Molloy's peculiarities, but does not add anything relevant to their essence. Anyway, there are some interesting points in Moran's report which hint at a progressive loss of mobility. Moran is a link between Molloy and Malone, between movement and definitive immobility. In Moran's account we thus find transitional elements. The most important of these elements, which Moran introduces and will then increasingly acquire importance in *Malone Dies* and in *The Unnamable*, is the voice he hears. "I have spoken of a voice giving me orders, or rather advice. It was on the way home I heard it for the first time. I paid no attention to it." (156) Moran hears a voice which gives him orders or, considering that he does not obey them, gives him advice. The mentioning of that voice and the definition of its purposes and limits is a development of Molloy's murmur hinting at changes (cf. *Molloy*, 81). The development can be shown by comparing a few sentences of the two characters. Molloy writes "I might doubtless have expressed otherwise and better, if I had gone to the trouble. And so I shall perhaps some day when I have less horror of trouble than today." (81) And Moran claims "I am still obeying orders, if you like, but no longer out of fear. No, I'm still afraid, but simply from force of habit." (121) Molloy's "horror of trouble" has become Moran's "force of habit".

How does Moran's voice work? He describes it on page 121.

> And the voice I listen to needs no Gaber to make it heard. For it is within me [...] Yes, it is rather an ambiguous voice and not always easy to follow, in its reasoning and decrees. But I follow it none the less, more

or less, I follow it in this sense, that I know what it means, and in this sense, that I do what it tells me. And I do not think there are many voices of which as much may be said.

The voice makes itself heard from within Moran and it is not easy to follow. Anyway Moran knows what it means and does what it tells him. There is a form of progress in that Moran has a specific willingness to cooperate with it. The voice is the most important force in Moran's account, it is what makes him write his report. The last words by Moran are:

> I have spoken of a voice telling me things. I was getting to know it better now, to understand what it wanted. It did not use the words that Moran had been taught when he was little and that he in his turn had taught to his little one. So that at first I did not know what it wanted. But in the end I understood this language. I understood it, I understand it, all wrong perhaps. That is not what matters. It told me to write the report. Does this mean I am freer now than I was? I do not know. I shall learn. Then I went back into the house and wrote, It is midnight. The rain is beating on the windows. It was not midnight. It was not raining. (162)

Moran claims that the voice does not use the words he has been taught and has taught his son, and that at first he had some difficulties in understanding it. Finally he understands it and writes the report. But he is not sure that he has understood it rightly, and in fact his report starts with two false statements, it is not midnight and it is not raining. Moran has, contrary to Molloy, the determination to understand the voice. He does not submit to a phenomenon he does not comprehend, he tries to understand the voice and consequently

Part III – "The Obligation to express"

does what it says.

Moran has no strong instincts as Molloy has, he does not "have the impression that" and nothing "seems to him that", his vision of the world is straightforward. Anyway, his behaviour does not prevent him from failing to report the voice, but his effort of will is a remarkable achievement. What is important, in this transition, is not the perfect understanding of the voice, but the act of trying to understand it. Moran has more consciousness of the voice than Molloy has.

His three kinds of movement, the physical, the mental and that of language, are thus influenced by this need to understand the voice. It is not necessary to analyse Moran's movement carefully because it is similar to Molloy's. Therefore I will only point out particularly interesting developments of ideas found in the first part of *Molloy*. Moran's physical journey starts and ends in his house. Its task is to find Molloy, but it is not a need, as it is for Molloy to find his mother; it is a duty he has to accomplish. Moran is used to that kind of duty and at the beginning he is not troubled. But he soon becomes so, when he sees that dealing with Molloy (only thinking of his name or of what he has to do when he finds him) causes him many problems. His physical journey to Ballybaba increasingly confuses his rational and precise mind; the nearer he gets to Molloy, the more similar to him he becomes. He even sits in the same way Molloy sits at the beginning of the novel. "I sat down with my back against a trunk, drew my feet up under me, took my legs in my arms and rested my chin on my knee." (125) Moran becomes instinctive and irrational. On page 150 he seems to have become crazy.

> I crawled out in the evening to have a good laugh at the lights of Bally. And though suffering a little from wind and cramps in the stomach I felt extraordinarily content, content with myself, almost elated, enchanted with my performance. [...] But Gaber's arrival put a

stop to these frolics.

From that point on to the end of his account, Moran slowly regains his rationality (his theological and practical questions, and his description of the bees' dance are two examples).

Moran's physical journey follows a crescendo which has its climax when he waits for death on page 150, and then decreases to the status described at the end of the novel. When Moran is nearest to Molloy, it is when he loses his rationality; when he is near to accomplishing his duty, Moran is not able to. This is a development of Molloy's relationship with his mother, for Moran does not need to meet Molloy in order not to be able to communicate, he simply needs to think of him. Moran shows how physical presence is no longer necessary to try to express something; he shows how the idea of the interlocutor is enough to provoke the (frustrated) attempt to communicate. It is a sort of useless movement. Moran travels to Ballybaba, but does not need to meet Molloy to establish a relationship with him (and in fact he goes to Ballybaba because it is an order and not because he wants to). Moran's pointless physical journey hints at Malone's and the unnamable's immobility.

Moran's mind has no instinctive impulses, if we exclude when he is near Bally, because his rationality is extremely powerful. Moran's life is perfectly structured by habits; if he fails to have communion he is not satisfied, if he does not eat at a definite time he becomes upset, etc. He has got all sorts of rules that order his life. Whatever is not completely under the control of rationality, he does not consider. He has a horror of his body and of its functions; he affirms that he does not like men nor animals and that God is beginning to disgust him, because he cannot control or rationalise them.

Molloy is the symbol of instinctive and irrational behaviour: he is in direct contrast with Moran. The encounter of the two (in Moran's mind) leads to a weakening of Moran's rationalistic view. The encounter provokes a definitive change. When Moran leaves

Ballybaba and goes back to his home, his rationality is not restored, but is contrasted by the voice speaking in his soul. Moran's mental journey begins by ignoring the lower and the higher levels (instinctive and spiritual), exasperating the rational one, inserts instinct in the middle, and ends by suggesting the introduction of the spiritual force.[59] There is a shift from Molloy, who has a strong instinct which has to submit to rationality, to Moran, who has a strong rationality which has to submit to the voice. Again Moran shows the direction in which the trilogy is moving; it is going towards a loss of instinct and rationality, leaving its Narrator with the difficulty of understanding spirituality.[60]

Moran's journey in language is similar to his mental one. At the beginning he has confidence in words. An example is his sentence on Father Ambrose. "Or of mental reservation as he pronounced the magic words." (94) He considers magic the words that transform bread and wine into the flesh and blood of Christ. Moran gives to the Father's words the power to transform and create something. Moran has a rationalistic faith, he believes in acts not in mental and spiritual inclination, but anyway, the importance he attaches to words is enormous.

When speaking of Molloy, Moran becomes confused about the power of words. "What I heard, in my soul I suppose, where the acoustics are so bad, was a first syllable, Mol, very clear, followed almost at once by a second, very thick, as though gobbled by the first, and which might have been oy as it might have been ose, or one, or even oc." (103) Language loses its foundation in rationality and founds it in spirituality; Moran is not sure of Molloy's name because he does not hear it clearly in his soul. Words, from magic, become unclear and no longer able to define and create a result. By the end of Moran's report, he restores the magic power of words, but in a destructive way. "And I recited the pretty quietist Pater, Our Father who art no more in heaven than on earth or in hell, I neither want nor desire that thy name be hallowed, thou knowest best what suits thee. Etc." (154) His Pater does not support his rationality but destroys it. The voice he hears contrasts with his rational belief in the power of words and creates a transitional destructive movement.

Malone's Immobility

The title of the second part of the trilogy shows by itself that Beckett is moving towards a complete standstill. Malone is lying in his bed and he is dying. His physical surroundings end where his room ends; his possessions are defined as those things "the whereabouts of which I know well enough to be able to lay hold of them" (229). Even his body is part of his physical surrounding and not of himself. "It is there I die, unbeknown to my stupid flesh." (171) Malone has taken refuge in his head so as to protect himself from "all the rest" (215) i.e. his useless body. Communication with anyone is impossible because he is voiceless and sometimes deaf. The only parts of his body he is in control of are his arms and his hands, which have an extension in the hooked stick.

Malone's immobility is broader than Molloy's or Moran's because he can no longer recall what happened before he was brought into the room.

> As to the events that led up to my fainting and to which I can hardly have been oblivious, at the time, they have left no discernible trace, on my mind. [...] But what is the last thing I remember, I could start from there, before I came to my senses again here? That too is lost. (168-9)

Malone cannot tell his story because he does not remember it.[61] Malone is dying and everything around him underlines that gradual shift towards an end of some kind. Habitual actions such as the arrival of the soup and the removal of his pot all cease; he does not hear any sound anymore.

In this physical stillness Malone tells his stories.[62] Ruby Cohn in his *Back to Beckett*, writes that "what *is* worth noting, Malone informs us early, are stories." (91) But we soon notice that Malone is not interested in plots; he is more concerned about his programme and his control over the stories themselves. He tells his stories to pass the time that remains for him to live and not because he has something important to say.[63] Malone's mind creates stories because it is waiting to become definitively silent. While waiting, he employs his rationality to invent something inessential, achieving the state of not having to focus his mind on himself. Malone longs for death because he is forgetting what life is; the memory of his direct experience is slowly fading.

How does Malone's mind operate in the creation of the stories he tells? At the beginning he sets up a programme. "I shall be able to tell myself four stories, each one on a different theme." (166) Then he describes what they will be about, reduces them to three and asks himself if he will have time to finish them. He concludes that if he does not finish, it does not matter, and if he finishes too soon he will make an inventory of his possessions.

When he seems to have exploited all possibilities, he asks himself if it would not be better to speak of his possessions first. "That is what reason counsels. But reason has not much hold on me, just now." (167) This sentence tells us that all these careful programmes are not to be considered too seriously because, although they seem so, they are not rational. Malone hints at it again a few lines later, when he resumes his programme. "To return to the five. Present state, three stories, inventory, there. An occasional interlude is to be feared. A full programme." (168) The interlude will be more than an occasional interruption, it will affect the stories, it will mix them up with Malone's own state and with the inventory of his possessions, it will prevent the conclusion of whatever part of Malone's programme. The interlude has to be understood as Malone's account of his rationality's awareness that death itself is nearing. The interlude is the part he prefers most because when it occurs it reminds him that the end is near.

The interlude contains the disturbing element which reminds us of the similar ones we have found in *Molloy*. Molloy has to submit to rationality, Moran is disturbed by the voice, Malone has to submit his inventions to the confusion of mental immobility. He tells the stories but is always aware that he is doing so in order to make his waiting less boring. This is the main difference between Molloy-Moran and Malone; the latter is already immobile but tries to galvanise his state for the last time, Molloy and Moran are moving in order to become motionless. Malone's mind cannot move backwards because it has forgotten everything that has happened. Not being able to speak of his past, Malone invents some movement to mix it with his motionless present. The interlude is something that can neither be considered part of the stories nor of Malone's "present state", and which takes Malone away from both of these two conditions of his mind.

> How are my plans getting on, my plans, I had plans not so long ago [...] I shall try and go on all the same, a little longer, my thoughts elsewhere, I can't stay here. I shall hear myself talking, afar off, from my far mind, talking of the Lamberts, talking of myself, my mind wandering, far from here, among its ruins. (198-9)

We are presented with an indefinite place, "here", which is not contained in the Narrator's mind and in which he is afraid to stay but which attracts him (cf. Part III, the sub-chapter on the unnamable). It is the description of that place, its effects on Malone, and his reactions that compose the interlude that Malone fears at the beginning

Part III – "The Obligation to express"

of his account. And, considering Malone's immobility, that interlude is the most important part of the novel because whenever it occurs (it interrupts the programme at regular intervals, but since Malone calls it "interlude" in the singular, I will do so too), we are made aware of his condition and of his attempts to escape from it. "I shall never go back into this carcass except to find out its time." (178) This is the first step taken by Malone to alienate himself from all source of movement; he does not want to dwell in his body anymore, and he will go back into it when it is time to leave it definitely. It is the rejection of the instinct the body contains (personified by Molloy). Although Malone can hardly move his body anymore, he shows a symbolic unwillingness to accept the force of instinct that moves the body. An example of this emotional response to events is to be found on page 217. "First I see the night, which surprises me, to my surprise, I suppose because I want to be surprised, just once more." But notice that Malone is *writing* those things; "I hear the noise of my little finger as it glides over the paper and then that so different of the pencil following after." (191) Malone carefully describes his pencils and his exercise-book.

> The first pages [of the exercise-book] are covered with ciphers and other symbols and diagrams, with here and there a brief phrase. Calculations, I reckon. They seem to stop suddenly, prematurely at all events. [...] I did not look closely. I drew a line no, I did not even draw a line, and I wrote, Soon I shall be quite dead at least, and so on, without even going on to the next page, which was blank. [...] The pencil on the contrary is an old acquaintance, I must have had it about me when I was brought here. It has five faces. It is very short. It is pointed at both ends. A Venus. (192)

Malone still depends on physical aspects although this dependence seems to be fading: he is writing with a pencil which is so short that "there is just room for my thumb and the two adjacent fingers, gathered together in a little vice." (204), and he writes "as lightly as [he] can" (204). These hints show that he wants and is forced to abandon every contact with physical aspects: and, in fact, he loses his exercise-book and his pencil.

> I fear I must have fallen asleep again. In vain I grope, I cannot find my exercise-book. But I still have the pencil in my hand. (191) [...] What a misfortune, the pencil must have slipped from my fingers, for I have only just succeeded in recovering it after forty-eight hours (see above) of intermittent efforts. (204)

And notice that Malone cares about his exercise-book: when the man who hits him on the head appears, Malone hides the exercise-book under the Blanket and then hides it somewhere else (248).

Malone's rationality, as we have already seen, is not meant to give a structure to his life (like Moran's), but is used to program his agony. But Malone does not rely on rationality, he uses it although he does not believe in its utility. He considers it a sort of mental disease. "I want, when the great day comes, to be in a position to enounce clearly, without addition or omission, all that its interminable prelude had brought me and left me in the way of chattels personal. I presume it is an obsession." (180) The actual development of his narration demonstrates his unwillingness (or his incapacity) to carry on what he had previously decided. His rationality is an attempt to create a diversion, to distract his attention from his immobility. Moran loses his rationality when he nears Molloy and regains it, albeit changed by the presence of the voice, when he leaves Ballybaba. Malone has already lost it at the beginning of the novel and revives it for a last time throughout the novel, because he still fears the silence of "here". He even revives instinct, in the episode of Big

Lambert. Malone's mind is not yet totally still, and thus he makes up programmes and invents stories, writing them because otherwise he will not be able to recall what he has already said. The product of Malone's rationality is not necessary for the comprehension of his character. In fact, he makes a clear distinction between his "present state" and his stories, from which he often turns away in disgust ("What tedium" and "What mortal tedium" are his refrains when commenting on the stories). Malone is aware that his speaking is meaningless ("What truth is there in all this babble?" introducing the idea that everything he says is just an involuntary product of his foolish mind), and he knows when, if it is the case, he will stop. "And if I ever stop talking it will be because there is nothing more to be said, even though all has not been said, even though nothing has been said." (216) In this passage Malone makes clear that the fact of becoming silent or not does not depend on rationality. He will stop his babble (product of his rationality) when he has lost interest in it (when there is nothing more to be said even though all has not been said), when he is absorbed by something else. If Moran's rationality is defeated by his instinct and by the voice respectively, Malone's rationality is defeated by itself, by its not being relevant anymore. This fact differentiates Malone from his two mobile predecessors, and makes it possible to define him as immobile. Through his control of the story of Sapo-Macmann he tries to demonstrate the omnipotence of his rationality.

> I stop everything and wait. Sapo stands on one leg, motionless, his strange eyes closed. The turmoil of the day freezes in a thousand absurd postures. The little cloud drifting before their glorious sun will darken the earth as long as I please. [...] All I ask is to know, before I abandon him whose life has so well begun, that my death and mine alone prevents him from living on, from winning, losing, joying, suffering, rotting and

dying (179-82)

It is the agony of Malone's rationality; like Moran, who wants to control his world, Malone needs to have control over his story. But he fails. The first reason is his bad memory. "Take his family, for example, I really know practically nothing about his family any more. But that does not worry me, there is a record of it somewhere. It is the only way to keep an eye on him." (190-1) The second and most important reason is that Malone often looks for Sapo-Macmann because he has lost him and Malone is not always sure that he is still speaking of the same person. "I have taken a long time to find him again, but I have found him. How did I know it was he, I don't know. (207-8) Can it be then that it is not the same Macmann at all, after all" (238). Furthermore, his characters change place without Malone's knowledge, and he is happy to find them where he has left them. "But for Macmann, thank God he's still there" (212). Malone finds both solutions interesting and amusing, he does not think that one should exclude the other, he carries them on at the same time. Omnipotence is mixed up with impotence to show how Malone's rationality is at an end; its last products are the death rattle which is heard from Malone's mind.

But if Malone's instinctive force has already disappeared and his rational one is dying, what about the spiritual one? How has Moran's voice developed in *Malone Dies*? Can it be considered immobile, too? Moran considers the ordering voice as exterior to himself (although he hears it through himself), Malone has already interiorised it and he considers it a part of himself. He does not hear nor try to understand it, he thinks of it as a place where he sometimes is. We are back to the passage mentioned on page 199. "I shall hear myself talking, afar off, from my far mind, talking of the Lamberts, talking of myself, my mind wandering, far from here, among its ruins." What Malone does not understand is found in that place he defines as "here."

Part III – "The Obligation to express"

Malone does not even try to understand the spiritual force, he submits to it when he cannot avoid it, and this is the only relationship he has with it. His stories are an attempt to escape from that place. "I had forgotten myself, lost myself. I exaggerate. Things were not going too badly. I was elsewhere. Another was suffering." (246) Malone is not only trying to entertain himself with stories, he is also trying to forget where he is (not his body nor his mind, but his spirit).

At a certain point, Malone attempts a great description of his feelings about that place. Malone becomes aware of its presence.

> And during all this time, so fertile in incidents and mishaps, in my head I suppose all was streaming and emptying away as through a sluice, to my great joy, until finally nothing remained, either of Malone or of the other. And what is more I was able to follow without difficulty the various phases of this deliverance and felt no surprise at its irregular course, now rapid, now slow, so crystal clear was my understanding of the reasons why this could not be otherwise. And I rejoiced furthermore, quite apart from the spectacle, at the thought that I now knew what I had to do, I whose every move has always been a groping, and whose motionlessness too was a kind of groping, yes, I have greatly groped stockstill. And here again naturally I was utterly deceived, I mean in imagining I had grasped at last the true nature of my absurd tribulations, but not so utterly as to feel the need to reproach myself with it now. For even as I said, How easy and beautiful it all is!, in the same breath I said, All will grow dark again. (205-6)

Malone describes the immobility of his mind which allows the advent of that new status of mind. This awareness is not omniscient, and it still can be misleading, but being a product of the emptying of Malone's mind, it is free of rationalistic influence. Or better, it should be, because Malone's rationality is in agony but not dead yet, and this causes the partial immobility of the spiritual force. He has an intuition ("I now knew what to do"), but he is not able to develop it ("And here again I was utterly deceived"). Anyway, he does not reproach himself again with these problems; he has the possibility, owing to his loss of memory, not to. If Molloy's spiritual journey is concerned with his inability to communicate with his mother (incommunication between two persons), and Moran's deals with the problems he has with the voice (incommunication between a person and an entity), Malone's spiritual journey concentrates on himself; with the weakening of his rationality he has discovered another part of his personality and tries to understand it.[64] He does not need to move either in space or in his mind; being immobile could be the better way to understand the third source.

The situation reaches an impasse. Malone, thanks to a partial loss of rationality, has experienced his spirituality and feels that in it he can "grasp the true nature of [his] absurd tribulations" (206). He is happy with this situation but also frightened by its novelty and vagueness. It is his rationality which strikes back. Malone is made unable to move by a rationality which does not work properly but still influences him, and by a spirituality which he shrinks from and of which, at the same time, he is unable not to feel the importance.[65]

What can Malone do? He can wait. In fact, he waits for (what he hopes will be) the definitive immobility which would release him from that tension i.e. death. Malone's language underlines the gradual loss of mobility. At the beginning it is strongly influenced by rationality. Malone is programming his last days and describing the possibilities he has. "I could die today, if I wished [...] I shall be neutral and inert. [...] I must be on my guard [...] I shall die tepid, without enthusiasm." (165) There are many examples, in the first few pages, of Malone's intentions and predictions of future events. When he starts to tell Sapo's story, his language changes and is dominated by his waiting for time to pass. His repeated comments on how the story proceeds ("What tedium" is the most common one) show how his use of language is moving towards a standstill because what he says does not absorb his attention and annoys him. Malone adds, to the physical obligation to write (Molloy), and to the spiritual obligation to understand the voice (Moran), his physical and spiritual indifference.

> Misfortune, blessings, I have no time to pick my words, I am in a hurry to be done, And yet no, I am in no hurry. Decidedly this evening I shall say nothing that is not false, I mean nothing that is not calculated to leave me in doubt as to my real intentions. (190)

If Molloy would just record the mere facts, and Moran would discuss this sentence from a rationalistic viewpoint, Malone does not care about what he is saying. His use of language concentrates on indifference.[66] Malone's account is monotonous, there is neither a rise nor fall in his use of language. Whether he speaks of himself, of Sapo-Macmann, of Big Lambert, or of something else, he does not understand, he is never troubled nor changed by what happens, by what his words may produce and cause, by what he says. His short memory prevents him from carrying on a homogeneous narration and it consequently causes the disinterest which is immobilising him.

To conclude this chapter and as an introduction to the next one, I would like to quote Malone once more.

> And it is a pleasure to find oneself again in the presence of one of those immutable relations between harmoniously perishing terms and the effect of which is this, that when weary to death one is almost resigned to - I was going to say to the immortality of the soul, but I

don't see the connexion. (210)

Malone is resigned to the immortality of the tension which has arisen from the confrontation of his rationality with his spirituality. He has not found a solution, he has been immobilised by this tension and now awaits death as a solution, a Hamletic to die - to sleep. His intuition, his resignation is right; he is going to be disappointed.

The Unnamable's Frustration

> I've swallowed three hooks and
> am still hungry. (*The Unnamable*, 311)

> And now let us think no more about
> it, think no more about anything, think
> no more. (309)

The Unnamable is the third and last part of Beckett's trilogy of novels. In it we find the end of those developments we have considered, starting with Molloy and passing on to Moran and Malone. The unnamable completes - or better, tries to complete - what has been left unfinished in the two previous novels. This sub-chapter considers how *The Unnamable* develops the results achieved in *Molloy* and in *Malone Dies*; it is followed by a sub-chapter in which I will try to give a structure to the whole trilogy and draw some conclusions.

The unnamable speaks from a place we have already encountered in *Malone Dies*, namely "here". This place is in opposition to "there" where he has never been but which has influenced, and still influences, him much. Malone occasionally finds himself "here", but he cannot bear to stay "here" for a long time. The unnamable is definitely "here" and does not want to be influenced by "there". "It is therefore permissible, in the light of this distant analogy, to think of myself as being here forever but not as having been here forever. [...] Did I wait somewhere for this place to be ready to receive me? " (271) This is a first contradiction. Has the unnamable always been "here" or has he also been "there" in some early stage of his existence? The answer is given on page 269. "I have been here, ever since I began to be, my appearances elsewhere having been put in by other parties." The unnamable has always been "here", but he has occasionally appeared elsewhere i.e. "there". Molloy, Moran, Malone, Basil, Mahood and Worm are the names he has been given when appearing "there".[67]

"Here" is a dark, vast, timeless place, but its description is misleading because the unnamable is not attaching any particular importance to it and consequently changes it from time to time.[68] What the unnamable is sure of is that "here" everything should be silent, calm, immobile; "all change to be feared, in comprehensible uneasiness." (271) "Here" is the place where the unnamable has become the unnamable; "here" is the only place where he identifies with himself. "I shall say therefore that our beginnings coincide, that this place was made for me, and I for it, at the same instant." (272) Molloy's roaming across Ballyba becomes Moran's journey Turdy-Ballybaba-Turdy, which becomes Malone's room, which becomes Mahood's jar, which becomes Worm's not knowing where he is, which becomes the unnamable's physically placeless, in some ways symbolic, "here".

But why, if the unnamable thinks that "here" should be an "unthinkable, unspeakable" (307) place, does he speak?[69] The first and most obvious answer is that he "cannot be silent" (269). The unnamable is speaking because he cannot stop, and would like to be silent because then he would be able to speak no more. He has no other aim. The reasons for his speaking are not material, he is not explaining that he is looking for a person (Molloy's mother, Molloy) or for something to happen (to understand the voice, to die); his purpose is totally abstract, he does not want to communicate, nor to accomplish a duty, nor to tell stories while waiting. Molloy has to write because a person obliges him to do it (in that he pays Molloy if he provides written material), Moran is spurred on by Gaber and by the voice he hears, Malone tells stories because he does not want to be bored and silent, but the unnamable has nothing to tell, he has no goal. He is forced to speak. He is not forced by a person, but by the influence a group of people has had on him at a previous stage.

> But I seem to have retained certain descriptions, in spite of myself. They gave me courses on love, on intelligence, most precious, most precious. They also taught me to count, and even to reason. Some of this rubbish has come in handy on occasions, I don't deny it, on occasions which would never have arisen if they had left me in peace. (273) I repeat they do not disturb me. But in the long run it might become wearisome. I don't see how. But the possibility must be taken into account. One starts things moving without a thought of how to stop them. In order to speak. One starts speaking as if it were possible to stop at will. (274)

The unnamable is aware that what they taught him has caused his inability to be silent by creating situations which he could not avoid coping with. The few paragraphs above contain many questions. From where is the unnamable speaking? What does he refer to when using the terms "here" and "there"? Has he always been "here"? Who are "they" who force him to speak? Why does he speak? What does he say? What would he like *not* to say? How is he developing what we have said about Molloy, Moran and Malone? Is he the end of the series? Is he completely immobile?

The unnamable is not speaking of himself and he is not in control of what he utters.

This voice that speaks, knowing that it lies, indifferent to what it says, too old perhaps and too abased ever to succeed in saying the words that would be its last, knowing itself useless and its uselessness in vain, not listening to itself but to the silence that it breaks (281)

The unnamable is interested in silence and he claims that he has no voice. "It's not mine, I have none, I have no voice and must speak, that is all I know" (281). He has some inkling of why he has to speak. "The thing to avoid, I don't know why, is the spirit of system." (268); "I who am here, who cannot speak, cannot think, and who must speak, and therefore perhaps think a little." (276); "What prevents the miracle [of going silent] is the spirit of method to which I have perhaps been a little too addicted." (278) The unnamable claims that speaking implies thinking and that he is prey to the use of rationality. He speaks, thus he has to think and is obliged to speak. It is a vicious circle but of a different kind from the ones we have already considered. The unnamable's problem is limited to having to speak-wanting to go silent, but there is no particular, practical reason.[70] Malone finds his words tedious and would like to be dead, but he does not question the process of speaking, over which he still has a certain power (he creates Sapo-Macmann and allows him to live). The unnamable has no power over what he says. "I'm a big talking ball, talking about things that do not exist, or that exist perhaps, impossible to know, beside the point." (280) He is not interested if his speech is true or not, or if it describes something; his problem is that he has to speak.

What does the unnamable say in his 120-page-long discourse? Is he narrating a story like his predecessors? Or is he complaining about his inability to go silent? He is doing both. Mahood and Worm are not two invented characters (like Sapo-Macmann for Malone); the unnamable confuses them with himself (when he tells Mahood's story he says "I"). He occasionally speaks with their voice ("To go on, I still call that on, to go on and get on has been my only care, if not always in a straight line, at least in obedience to the figure assigned to me, there was never any room in my life for anything else. Still Mahood speaking." 294). He suggests that he could be Mahood ("Or the admission that I am Mahood after all and these stories of a being whose identity he usurps, and whose voice he prevents from being heard, all lies from beginning to end?" 285), and he even questions his being "here" ("What if we were one and the same after all, as he affirms and I deny? And I been in the places where he says I have been, instead of having stayed on here, trying to take advantage of his absence to unravel my tangle?" 289). This last quote suggests some parallelism with Biblical versions of the unsayable and unnamable; notice the similarities with Jesus speaking with the voice of God e.g. John 8:58 "Jesus said unto them, Verily, verily I say unto you, Before Abraham was, I am".

The fictional presence of Mahood, his relationship with the unnamable ("I don't know how it was done. I always liked not knowing, but Mahood said it wasn't right." 283), and the unnamable's identification with him enable the latter to transform the former into a character that roams up and down the series of people we have already mentioned. Mahood is similar to Molloy and Moran when he travels home and finds his family lying dead on the floor, and he is similar to Malone, or rather develops some of his features, when he is contained in the jar.[71] In fact, Mahood is not noticed by anyone, not even by dogs or flies and his keeper, although she looks after him, doubts his existence.

Malone does not belong to the world anymore in that he is confined to a room but he has contact sparingly with the outside world (although it constantly decreases and by the end of his account stops; he does not hear sounds anymore, he cannot turn his head to look out of the window, nobody enters the room). Mahood is noticed by one person only, and at the end of Mahood's story, she is convinced that he actually does not exist. The unnamable's account of Mahood's story starts with movement ("I was under the impression I spent my life in spirals round the earth." 300), and ends with immobility at a metaphoric "very brink of the precipice" (306) where Mahood stands with no hope of change because he is already dead. "It's usually with sticks they put me out of their agony, the idea being to demonstrate, to the backers, and bystanders, that I had a beginning and an end." (306) The unnamable re-absorbs Mahood when he has used him to show to the readers that he is setting forth Moran's and Malone's stories. "Before Mahood there were others like him, of the same breed and creed, armed with the same prong." (310) In his direct account the unnamable summarises what we have considered in the previous chapters; from page 307 to the end of the novel, Mahood will appear, mingled with the unnamable, to add elements to the status Malone has reached. In fact, Mahood is the element that joins the unnamable with "there". "All of a sudden a horse will neigh. Then I'll know that nothing has changed." (316-7) It is Mahood's last effort to convince the unnamable of their similarity, to persuade him that he too lives "there" but does not realise it. But the unnamable is aware of that effort. "The stories of Mahood are ended. He has realised they could not be about me, he has abandoned, it is I who win [...] To make me believe I have an ego all of my own, and can speak of it, as they of theirs. Another trap to snap me up among the living." (317) Mahood exploits his duty to bridge certain gaps between Malone and the unnamable, he makes clear for the readers what has happened between the end of *Malone Dies* and the beginning of *The Unnamable*.

At this point, the unnamable transforms Mahood into Worm.

> Worm is the first of his kind. [...] He has not yet been able to speak his mind, only murmur, I have not ceased to hear his murmur, all the while the other discoursed.

(310) what can I say of Worm, who hasn't the wit to make himself plain? (311)

The Narrator of the trilogy has to pass through Worm to reach the unnamable ("Or if I am not yet Worm, I shall be when I cease to be Mahood" 310). Worm is a character who is not in possession of the distinctive features that a dweller of "there" should have; a first one, as already seen, is that he is not able to understand his mind. A second is that "Worm cannot note" (312).[72] The third is that he does not exist.

> Worm, to say he does not know what he is, where he is, what is happening, is to underestimate him. What he does not know is that there is anything to know. His senses tell him nothing, nothing about himself, nothing about the rest, and this distinction is beyond him. Feeling nothing, knowing nothing, he exists nevertheless, but not for himself, for others, other conceive him and say, Worm is, since we conceive him, as if there could be no being but being conceived, if only by the beer. (318)

Worm exists if someone conceives him and with that purpose only. He is a sort of puppet who can be filled by the one who has conceived him. But the fact that he exists makes it inevitable that he contains something and thus that he has an aim to accomplish (otherwise he would not have been conceived). Worm is the last step before we reach "here", where the unnamable is. Neither has a body, neither thinks, and they both speak without knowing what they say. "Is there a single word of mine in all I say? No, I have no voice, in this matter I have none. That's one of the reasons why I confuse myself with Worm. But I have no reason either, no reason, I'm like Worm, without voice or reason" (319). Worm has a body, he has thoughts, he speaks and acts "there", but all these phenomena exist only because someone conceives them; the unnamable has no body, he does not act "there", but he still expresses thoughts and utters words.

The unnamable is the first character of the series who is conscious and happy to be "here". From "here" he has followed, or maybe interpreted, Murphy, Watt, Mercier, Camier, Molloy, Moran, Malone, Mahood and Worm; but he "never desired, never sought, never suffered, never partook in any of that, never knew what it was to have, things, adversaries, mind, senses." (299)

"Here" is a place where instincts, rationality, objects and people do not exist, it is even not a calm place of silence ("the silence is outside, outside, inside, there is nothing but here" 378), it is simply "here". A place where "I can't rejoice and I can't grieve, it's in vain they explained to me how it's done, I never understood" (324), and where the unnamable does not even have an identity, "the confusion of identities being merely apparent and due to my inaptitude to assume any." (303) "Here" is the realm of detachment from whatever excess, it is a state of balance between opposing forces and influences.[73] "Here" is the neatness opposed to the disorder of "there"; complete, timeless immobility opposed to unforeseeable movement; a clear vision opposed to the tricks of illusion.

The unnamable is disturbed at his being "here". He is detached ("As far as I personally am concerned there is every likelihood of my being incapable of ever desiring or deploring anything whatsoever." 346), but he is not safe from disorder, movement and illusion. His narration is an account of what prevents him from being immune to confusion. The unnamable has always been "here", even though he knows many things that belong "there". The reason is that there are people who "take themselves for me" (288), who condemn the unnamable for being in contact with "there". Those people are the protagonists of the two novels that precede *The Unnamable* in the trilogy, Molloy, Moran, Malone, and, in the last part, Mahood and

Worm.⁷⁴ They try to divert the unnamable from "here" and transfer him "there". The first quote at the beginning of this sub-chapter ("I've swallowed three hooks and am still hungry") refers to Molloy's Moran's and Malone's attempts. The unnamable does not give in to their endeavours, although sometimes he is tempted to.

> [W]hat they want, they want me to be, this, that, to howl, stir, crawl out of here, be born, die, listen (355) is it the return to the world of fable, no, just a reminder, to make me regret what I have lost, long to be again in the place I was banished from, unfortunately it doesn't remind me of anything. (375) perhaps that's how I'll find silence, and peace at last, by opening my doors and letting myself be devoured, they'll stop howling, they'll start eating, the maws now howling. Open up, open up, you'll be all right, you'll see. (360)

In these three passages we have three different kinds of being re-absorbed by "there". The first one concerns instinct, the second is about language (cf. Part II, the chapter on Vico) and the third one concerns rationality (on this occasion called "they").

"Here" the unnamable has no instinctive behaviour. The only natural tendency he has is towards total silence and peace. Being bodiless and thoughtless (the words he speaks are not his, he claims on several occasions), he cannot act (nor react) by a natural ability. Mahood in his linking Malone with the unnamable, shows a gradual loss of instinct.

> Yes, it was fatal, no sooner had the tarpaulin settled over me, and the precipitate steps of my benefactress died away, than the tears began to flow. In this, was this to be interpreted as an effect of gratitude? But in that case should I not have felt grateful? (301)

Mahood's body reacts in one way and his mind in another. Like Moran and Malone, Mahood does not understand and loses control over his body, but he is not worried by this fact. Mahood's lack of interest in linking his body and his mind is symptomatic of the absence of these two elements in the unnamable.

The unnamable's relationship with language is controversial; on the one hand he uses it and on the other he claims that it is not himself who is speaking.

> I add this, to be on the safe side. These things I say, and shall say, if I can, are no longer, or are not yet, or never were, or never will be, or if they were, if they are, if they will be, were not here, are not here, will not be here, but elsewhere. (276) Nothing then but me, of which I know nothing, except that I have never uttered (278)

The unnamable denies every bond between what he is and what he says ("I'll speak of me when I speak no more" 361), but he speaks because he is looking for something. "[I]t is in fact required of me that I say something, something that is not to be found in all I have said up to now." (285) The unnamable is forced to speak and in what he says he searches for something that will enable him to stop. Malone is annoyed by his stories but he tells them because he has to wait; he is annoyed by their content but not by their being stories; the unnamable has no more contact with words, he finds them useless and even harmful.[75]

> [I]t's to go silent that you need courage, for you'll be punished, punished for having gone silent, and yet you can't do otherwise than go silent, than be punished for having gone silent, than be punished for having been

punished, since you begin again (363)

What is the punishment for the unnamable who tries to go silent? "[M]y crime is my punishment," he claims on page 339. Like Dante's Conte Ugolino, who gnaws the archbishop Ruggieri's neck in order to be punished for his cannibalism involving his sons and nephews (Inf., xxxii, 123 - xxxiii, 78), the unnamable's punishment for trying to go silent consists in having to speak.[76]

The unnamable is a channel which reports words suggested by someone else. If Molloy has forgotten how to spell and has forgotten "half the words" (9), the unnamable uses words of which he does not know, and has never known, the meaning. "I say aporia without knowing what it means" (267), and on page 375:

> perhaps it's springtime now, that's all words they taught me, without making their meaning clear to me, that's how I learnt to reason, I use them all, all the words they showed me, there were columns of them, oh the strange glow all of a sudden, they were on lists, with images opposite, I must have forgotten them, I must have mixed them up, these nameless images I have, these imageless names

The unnamable has not directly experienced the things he speaks of, and thus he confuses objects and definitions. Words, for him, are completely detached from objects and vice versa, and he is detached from both. The Narrator's relationship with language, and his relationship with instinct, reach their peak with the unnamable; there is no point of contact, incomprehension, lack of consciousness, and lack of knowledge of their existence. If we simply consider these two relationships the unnamable could be regarded as close to what we have defined as self-realisation, near to uncovering the *unknown*.

But what prevents the disclosure of what the unnamable longs for is "their" presence. "They" are the unnamable's enemies. "I can see them still, my delegates." (272) "They" obey a master who has complete power over them. "They" can be meant to stand for different things on different levels. On a first literal level "they" may stand for the series of characters the unnamable, or rather, the Narrator has enacted, and who come back to disturb him with the memory of their previous existence, Molloy, Moran, Malone, but also Murphy, Mercier, and others, who haunt the unnamable with their problems and hinder his search for silence.

On a second level "they" may stand for rationality. The unnamable is conscious that if he uses rationality he will go back "there". "[M]y mind at peace, that is to say empty." (285) One condition for realising peace is not having his mind troubled by rationality. But rationality (which the unnamable considers separate from himself, too) constantly tries to swallow him up.

> They have told me, explained to me, described to me, what it all is, what it looks like, what it's all for, one after the other, thousand of times, in thousand of connections, until I must have begun to look as if I understood. [...] What I speak of, what I speak with, all comes from them. (297)

Rationality tries to overwhelm the unnamable by insisting, by filtering every event and phenomenon through itself, in a sort of continuous temptation. What protects the unnamable is the fact that he does not understand a rationalistic vision. "Dear incomprehension, it's thanks to you I'll be myself, in the end." (298) The pressure of rationality is constant and subtle, and the unnamable is confused by it. He desperately claims "let him [the master] inform me once and for all what exactly he wants from me, for me." (287) There is no direct and clear answer, "their" whispering continues and the unnamable has to cope with it. Sometimes, especially towards the end of the novel, rationality nearly reaches its goal. "The place I'll make it all the same, I'll make it in my head, I'll draw it out of my memory, I'll gather it all about me, I'll make myself a head, I'll make myself a memory, I have only to listen, the voice will tell me everything," (378-9) or, as in the following quotation, where the unnamable mixes the knowledge of rational influence on him and a rationalistic comment ("that's coherent"). "[B]ut it's not my turn to know what, to know what I am, where I am, and what I should do to stop being it, to stop being there, that's coherent, so as to be another, no, the same, I don't know, depart into life" (379).

The unawareness of the presence and use of rationality mingles with the refusal and inability to understand its purpose. "I was entirely absorbed in the business on hand and not at all concerned to know precisely, or even approximately, what it consisted in." (293) The unnamable reacts to that frustration in two opposite ways. On the one hand (as already seen for language) he complies with rationality in order to achieve what rationality wants from him, although he does not know what it is:

> so that they may be pleased with me, and perhaps leave me in peace at last, and free to do what I have to do, namely try and please the other, if that is what I have to do, so that he may be pleased with me, and leave me in peace at last, and give me quittance, and the right to rest, and silence, if that is in his gift. (307)

On the other hand, he tries to get rid of the influence of rationality.

> The voice. I hardly hear it any more. I'm going silent. Hearing the voice no more, that's what I call going silent, That is to say I'll hear it still, if I listen hard. I'll listen hard. Listening hard, that's what I call going

silent. I'll hear it still, broken, faint, unintelligible, if I listen hard. Hearing it still, without hearing what it says, that's what I call going silent. [...] Hearing too little to be able to speak, that's my silence. (362)

The unnamable does not understand why neither his attempt to accomplish what rationality wants from him nor his attempt to exclude it from his existence, enable him to be silent. His predecessors seem to have poisoned him irremediably with their ordering rationality. Moran's destructive rationality (cf. the already quoted Pater, *Molloy*, 154) is contrasted with the voice, which is equally powerful; Molloy's rationality is often silenced by his instinct; Malone's mind is semi-obstructed by his inability to remember but is still used to create stories; but the unnamable, having no instincts nor memories, living completely detached from the physical world, is not able to cope with that intrusion. "*De nobis ipsis silemus*," he affirms on page 302. The unnamable does not speak of what he is concerned about, he never speaks of himself.[77]

It is here that the unnamable gets caught up in a vicious circle; he would like to express something personal, something that has to do with his essence, but rationality makes it impossible with its continuous disturbance. The unnamable suspects that the voice of rationality is desperately trying to hold on ("I'd demand no more of me than to know that what I hear is not the innocent and necessary sound of dumb things constrained to endure, but the terror-stricken babble of the condemned to silence." 326), and so he tries to overcome that hindrance and postpones the expression of what he is interested in to the defeat of rationality. "For them it's the end, for me the beginning" (353).[78] But rationality can only be defeated by a force that replaces it.

The unnamable has understood that it is not rationality that interests him, but has not yet understood what exactly he seeks in silence. "[B]ut there are still certain depths we prefer not to sink to" he claims on page 345, but he adds "Let us keep to the familiar circle, it's more intimate, we all know one another now, no surprises to be feared, the will has been opened, nothing for anybody." Rationality is dead for the unnamable, and it does not bequeath him anything, even though he prefers not to leave it because he already knows it.

The unnamable prefers not to sink to certain depths because he does not know what he will discover. What paralyses the unnamable is his indecision; he does not leave something that no longer means anything to him but to which he is accustomed (rationality), and he does not accept something that attracts him but with which he is still not acquainted (spirituality).

> [T]hat's the show, someone reciting, selected passages, old favourites, a poetry matinée, or someone improvizing, you can barely hear him, that's the show, you can't leave, you're afraid to leave, it might be worse elsewhere, [...] that's the show, waiting for the show, [...] that's the show, waiting alone, in the restless air, for it to begin, for something to begin, for there to be something else but you, for the power to rise, the courage to leave, you try and be reasonable, perhaps you are blind, probably deaf, the show is over, all is over, [...] that's the show, free, gratis and for nothing, waiting alone, blind deaf, you know where, you don't know for what, for a hand to come and draw you away, somewhere else, where perhaps it's worse. (351)

The unnamable is waiting for a hand to come and draw him away, he does not realise that it is himself that has to lead his departure from the show, from the realm of rationality. What he is looking for is a new pure conscious self.

The unnamable's reactions to his inability to reach the depths of his inner being are the consequence of his two strategies for dealing with rationality. On the one hand he reacts violently, as in the long passage where he refers to himself as "a caged beast born of caged beasts" (356, but the passage continues for nearly two pages), and on the other hand he mingles desperation, hope and resignation:

> perhaps they have said me already, perhaps they have carried me to the threshold of my story, before the door that opens on my own story, that would surprise me, if it opens, it will be I, it will be the silence, where I am, I don't know, I'll never know, in the silence you don't know, you must go on, I can't go on, I'll go on. (381-2)

The Unnamable ends and nothing has changed since its beginning, the Narrator does not undergo any change in the course of the novel. He waits, endlessly postponing what he cares about. In the two previous parts of the trilogy we have witnessed the gradual loss of power of all sources except the spiritual one, which increasingly haunts the Narrator. In *The Unnamable*, we are presented with a standstill since the Narrator is already detached from instinct, rationality, language. But he is not yet absorbed by the force he recognises to be the only one which absorbs all his interest.

An Attempt to Give a Structure to the Trilogy

In the following table I have summarised the relations between characters and forces in the trilogy.

	Molloy	Moran	Malone	Mahood	Worm	unnamable
Physical Movement	++	+	-, but he moves his arms	--, for a while his head moves up and down in the jar	---, he falls because of the force of gravity	---
Linguistic Movement	a man compels him to write / he forgets the meaning of words	Gaber and the voice compel him to write / the importance of words changes after he hears the voice	powerful	---, he talks in order to bring the unnamable back "there"	---	---, but rationality obliges him to use it
Mental Movement: Instinct	powerful	has horror of	revives in imagination with the story of Big Lambert	---, even animals do not notice his existence	---, he does not exist	---

Mental Movement: Rationality	sometimes overwhelms instinct	powerful	revives for a last time	---	---	---, but it haunts him
Mental Movement: Spirituality	pushes him to look for his mother	the voice upsets his rational view of the world	longs for a definitive change, i.e. death	---	---, but his not knowing that there is anything to know nears him to the unnamable's silence	powerful, but he has not the courage to accept it

Table 1. Forces and movement in the trilogy.

It is interesting to read the table horizontally, taking into consideration the development of the different forces.

With regard to movement, from Molloy to the unnamable we are presented with a descending climax. Molloy's life is based on rambling (disorderly movement), Moran is mobile but only if he has to be (ordered movement), Malone is immobile but for his arms and occasionally would like to move, Mahood performs a vertical movement in his jar, Worm moves only if someone conceives him moving, and the unnamable is immobile and immovable.

The relationship between characters and language can be considered as dual. On the one hand, there is the interaction between the characters and the physical act of writing, and on the other hand we have to consider how much the characters are familiar with the meaning of words. The first kind of reaction is, for Molloy, mechanical; a man pays him if he writes and thus he fills pages. Moran is pushed to write by Gaber and by the voice (man and force), Malone strongly needs to write (force), but it is impossible to understand how the unnamable manages to write. The meaning of words is more and more unclear for Molloy; it changes radically for Moran after he has heard the voice; Malone uses words in a standardised way although he is sometimes confused; Mahood speaks to bring the unnamable back "there"; Worm is silent, and the unnamable is not interested in what rationality says through him. Words become a deficient means of expression which tries to describe an unsayable subject.

Instinct is very powerful in Molloy, it is thwarted by Moran, it is virtually non-existent in Malone and it is missing in Mahood, Worm and the unnamable.

Rationality is present and occasionally overwhelms instinct in Molloy, it is remarkably present in Moran, it is brought back into use for a last time by Malone, it is absent in Mahood and Worm, its recollection still haunts the unnamable.

The last force, spirituality, operates occasionally in Molloy and it pushes him to find his mother; it is heard by Moran as the voice; it draws Malone's attention to what he thinks to be the definitive parting from the other forces i.e. death; it could be present in Worm's silence; and finally it is what the unnamable is interested in.

To conclude. The trilogy starts with mobility and moves towards a total standstill. All the forces we have considered reach a climax during the two first novels and fall in *The Unnamable*, the only exception being what we have called spirituality. But what does spirituality mean for the unnamable, or rather for the Narrator, who leads us through the four parts and ends nameless? What is he looking for when he longs for silence in his "being here"? The Narrator is looking for himself, he tries to eliminate all elements that divert him from reaching a perfect consciousness of himself. This mechanism is highly spiritual, cf. *Bhagavad Gita*: "[w]hen your intelligence has passed out of the dense forest of delusion, you shall become indifferent to all that has been heard and all that has to be heard." (140) As we have seen, the unnamable tries to do it but at the end of the novel has not yet succeeded. The reason is that "[t]he senses are so strong and impetuous, O Arjuna, that they forcibly carry away the mind even of a man of discrimination who is endeavouring to control them." (148) But whoever is able to control them, Krishna adds, establishes a fulfilled consciousness. The Narrator's quest is of a mystical nature; by looking inward he tries to reach and unify himself with the totality of events.

Beckett's trilogy may be considered, among other things, the chronicle of an approach to the knowledge that self-consciousness is an important task in every man's existence. Beckett presents the difficulties a researcher may encounter and, in the course of his three novels, he describes different stages of control over the forces that hinder self-consciousness. Beckett's interest lies in that research and not in its results. This is the reason why the Narrator is still striving to find a solution at the end of *The Unnamable*. Beckett has not found an answer. Beckett's mastery is that of being able to capture and render these moments of tension without simplifying them by means of theories or by means of an easy way-out. He concentrates on an element without laying the others aside. He chooses to tackle one particular relation at a time (as seen in Table 1), but, like a real researcher, he has to cope with all the various forces at the same time. The trilogy leads to involvement in that it presents mechanisms and difficulties every researcher into self-awareness is confronted with, and not because it shows a solution to the problems it sets out. The trilogy can be defined as an "on the road" book, where the road is that of spiritual research and the possible, future destination is that of existence, knowledge and bliss.

DRAMA: BECKETT'S ALLEGORY AND HIS USE OF THE ABSURD

In the previous chapter we have seen how much Beckett is interested in mechanisms; the fact that he is looking for something is more important than what he is actually searching for. Molloy, Moran, Malone and the unnamable carefully describe how they try to reach what they feel they have to and, although they interpret that need on different levels, they never succeed in satisfying it. The progressive development of the trilogy is useful in that it shows that, although the aim changes from one character to the other, the need is always the same; and it also demonstrates that up to the end of *The Unnamable*, the aims suggested are not complementary to the force. Beckett's characters ordain their defeat by concentrating on something that is not able to quench their thirst for knowledge. It is this impossible source-aim relation that throws the reader into confusion because he senses the difference between them, but he cannot name it. The reader of the trilogy perceives the greatness of the force that haunts the Narrator, and at the same time is conscious of the partiality of the solutions suggested by different characters.

This chapter concentrates on that tension, with stress on the source. I will concentrate on Beckett's (non-)usage of allegorical actions and on his creating works that have been defined as "absurd". Trying to give a more precise account of the term "absurd", in the first part of this chapter I will analyse and attempt to set out some ideas found in Wolfgang Hildesheimer's article "Über das absurde Theater". This article was written in 1960, but is still very useful to understand how absurd plays and novels work. In the second part, I will concentrate on *Endgame* and on the tension that arises during the performance of the play.

Wolfgang Hildesheimer's "Absurde Theater"

Hildesheimer starts by suggesting why absurd theatre is useful. "Das absurde Theater dient der Konfrontation des Publikums mit dem Absurden, indem es ihm seine eigene Absurdität vor Augen führt." (13) But what does Hildesheimer mean by "absurd"? He claims that an absurd play is a particular kind of parable. The normal parable is created by an author who knows the indirect statement the story hints at,

> während das absurde Theaterstück eben dürch das absichtliche Fehlen jegliche Aussage zu einer Parabel des Lebens wird. Denn das Leben sagt ja auch nichts aus. Im Gegenteil: es stellt eine permanente, unbeantwortete Frage, so würde der Dramatiker des Absurden argumentieren, zöge er es nicht vor, sein Argument in die Parabel eines Theaterstückes zu kleiden, das die Konfrontation des Menschen mit der ihm fremden Welt - also mit der Frage - zum Thema hat. (15)

The absurd parable, Hildesheimer claims, is an accomplished written text which teaches an unaccomplishable, infinite lesson. It is an allegory for man's attitude towards life, the defined, little human being confronted with the unforeseen, limitless events that life presents. It is thus the sum of all absurd works that suggests the allegorical meaning of the parable, and each part shows a different aspect of the same whole.

But absurd theatre is not only an attempt to show a particular little part of life, it is also an effort made to grasp the whole.

> [D]as absurde Stück konfrontiert den Zuschauer mit der Unverständlichkeit, der Fragwürdigkeit des Lebens. Die Unverständlichkeit des Lebens kann aber nicht

> durch den Versuch einer Antwort dargestellt werden, denn das würde bedeuten, dass sie interpretierbar, das Leben also verständlich wäre. Sie kann nur dadurch dargestellt werden, dass sie sich in ihrer ganzen Grösse und Erbarmungslosigkeit enthüllt und quasi als rethorische Frage im Raum steht: wer auf eine Deutung wartet, wartet vergebens. Er wird sie nicht erhalten, bis er von kompetenter Seite den Sinn der Schöpfung erklärt bekommt, also nie. (17)

We have already seen in the chapters about the trilogy how Beckett starts from that point of view (e.g. Molloy's looking for his mother) but ends differently. The unnamable tries to find a comprehensive answer to his doubts; his longed-for silence is a refusal to accept the confusion of life in favour of an omniscient and ordering overview. The unnamable's outlook is not totally able to reject life's confusion, neither is he able to order it in a harmonious way; he tries to overcome disorder by means of pure rationality, which is part of that disorder. The unnamable reaches an impasse at a level slightly higher than the one suggested by Hildesheimer; though he has rejected life's confusion in favour of an ordering self-consciousness, he fails to apply it because he is not able to abandon the forces that rule that confusion.

Why does an author write absurd plays? Hildesheimer affirms that

> [d]er absurde Dramatiker vertritt die Ansicht, dass kein Kampf der Welt jemals auf dem Theater ausgefochten worden ist, dass das Theater noch keinen Menschen geläutert und keinen Zustand verbessert hat, und sein Werk zieht - je nach Veranlagung seines Autors - bittere oder komische Konsequenzen aus dieser Tatsache. (22-3) Der Dramatiker des Absurden, der kein Referat

zu halten hat, analysiert ja nicht, sondern schreibt Stücke und wartet höchstens - wie Ionesco - darauf, dass man sie ihm erkläre. (23)

The author does not write because he thinks that his work will improve the world; he writes without asking himself too many questions about what he is writing. This happens because he knows that every single play cannot be explained if the audience accepts the fact that it is absurd. *Waiting for Godot*, for example, has been interpreted in various ways by different audiences and critics but Beckett has repeatedly claimed that there is no particular explanation but the play itself.

The only explanation, Hildesheimer claims, is that the audience acknowledges the existence and power of the absurd. But, I would like to add, recognising the absurd is not a passive act; it is not possible to merely record it without any reaction. The duty of the absurd is, by means of its absurdity, to spur the audience on to global search. From the particular, absurd problem (e.g. will Godot come?) the audience ascends to more general levels (e.g. why are Didi and Gogo waiting? why do they need to wait? why do they always come back to the country road?) and finally translates these questions about the play into personal ones (e.g. who is my personal Godot? what do I have to do to contact him? how can I overcome the standstill presented in the play?).

Absurd theatre, exactly because it is absurd, cannot be explained literally nor allegorically. But in order to translate its meaning into an intelligible language, the audience has to become aware of the force the author has complied with.

Ionesco's introduction to *Stühlen* (quoted in Hildesheimer's "Über das absurde Theater") contains the same idea. "Dieses Gefühl der Unwirklichkeit, die Suche nach einer wesentlichen, vergessenen, unbenannten Realität, ausserhalb derselben ich nicht zu sein glaube, wollte ich ausdrücken " (16-7). What is important, what the author tries to attain is that "wesenliche, vergessene, unbenannte Realität". But since Beckett has not reached it in the play he has written, since he has only been able to hint at it, he gives his characters the freedom of choosing how and if to act. Didi's and Gogo's indecision outlasts the end of the play; the audience is left wondering whether they will leave and whether Godot will come. The play ends, but a solution is still possible, nothing is definitive. Didi and Gogo do not develop their characteristics in the course of the play, but they have the potentiality to. It is because of this aspect that Beckett's theatre differentiates itself from his trilogy of novels, his plays present no development. In the trilogy we have the possibility, passing from one character to the other, to be aware of a change; in *Waiting for Godot*, the brief amount of time in which the plot takes place is inadequate for any change to be noticed. The spectators feel the power contained in the play and find it in contrast with the condition of no movement and no activity described on stage; from that tension stems the idea that something may happen after the curtain has been drawn. Hildesheimer affirms that

> [d]ie Kunst des absurden Theaters liegt ja nicht darin, dem Publikum den Weg zu ebnen, ihm eine Eselsbrücke von der Wirklichkeit hinüber ins Unwirkliche, Surreale, Groteske zu bauen, indem sie die Wirklichkeit behutsam und allmählich abwandelt. (21)

The theatre of the absurd does not present a particular theme on which the audience can meditate, but it presents a situation from which the audience has to start. Beckett in his "Dante...Bruno.Vico..Joyce" writes that "His [Joyce] writing is not *about* something; *it is that something itself.*"(*Disjecta*, 27)

Beckett's theatre can be described by developing this statement. Beckett's "that something itself" is so vast that, as we have already seen, he can only describe how he tries to realise it, and his frustration when he is not able to. But in the words he writes, there are all the elements that make possible that realisation; they contain the essence of that search. The audience feels it, and it understands that the words pronounced, although their meaning is confused (but what search is easy?), *are* "that something itself".

Communication and Moments of Tension in *Endgame*

> My work is a matter of fundamental sounds (no joke intended) made as fully as possible, and I accept responsibility for nothing else.
> (*Disjecta*, 109)

Endgame seems very similar to *Godot*: in both plays the audience is confronted with two couples who have nothing to do, the setting is limited to a narrow place, there is no apparent plot, the characters are old. But the great difference between the two plays is that if *Godot* refuses to end (Godot never arrives), *Endgame* refuses to start; Hamm first sentence (which is the play's first line) states it clearly: "Finished, it's finished, nearly finished, it must be nearly finished." This is one of the reasons why *Endgame* can be considered one of Beckett's best plays; the audience is confronted with something new: why are the people sitting in a theatre if the play is over? The audience is a sort of *voyeur* who is waiting for something which has already ended. Hamm's words "[t]he end is in the beginning and yet you go on" (69) gives us an idea about the circular structure of the play; it begins but it has already ended, it cannot end because it has never begun. "*Endgame* represents life governed by the consciousness of endings as imminent in beginnings" (Bersani, 40). In *Endgame* Beckett uses very few elements that divert the audience from what he is hinting at. Hamm, Clov, Nagg and Nell do not wait for anyone or anything, they are not troubled about how to act, their future does not depend on anything. *Endgame* is a play in which nothing happens, the only action being the words spoken by Hamm, Clov, Nagg and Nell.

The tension that arises in the course of the play is thus purely verbal. Beckett has developed, in *Endgame*, an aspect that we have not yet discussed: that of the relationships between characters. Molloy, Moran, Malone and the unnamable do not interact (or very sparingly) with other people. Being concentrated on themselves, trying to reach a different degree of self-consciousness, they are unable to set up an exchange of ideas and opinions with anyone else. In *Endgame*, apparently, it is different because the play is composed of long dialogues. Hamm and Clov, instead of representing the reality of the spectator, claim that illusion is always hunting them, and then they imitate reality with words in order to be able to show, later in the play, that it is an illusion and that what they experience is different. In this sub-chapter we will analyse the play, proceeding on two levels; the first one is the play itself, with its relationships between the characters; and the second one is concerned with the connection between the audience and the stage. This second level is as important as the first one; the relationship between the spectators and the actors shows to what extent Beckett is able to communicate what he sets out to achieve.

The analyses will focus on communication and then on a particular moment of it, that of tension, when two characters (or a character and the audience) are at loggerheads.

There are three different couples who verbally interact, Hamm with Clov, Hamm with Nagg and Nagg with Nell. Added to these, there is the explicit relationship between some characters (Hamm and Clov) and the audience, to which the last part of this sub-chapter will be dedicated.

Between Hamm and Clov there is a relationship of mutual interdependence though Hamm has more authority; he is the master of the shelter and that is why he can give orders (but also because of his blindness and his immobility in the wheel-chair.) Every time Hamm commands, Clov obeys, also if the order is contradictory. HAMM "Then it's not worth while opening it?" CLOV "No." HAMM (*violently.*) "Then open it!" (*Clov gets up on the ladder, opens the window.*) (43)

Clov needs his presence, he hates him, he wants to leave him but he is not able to, as he declares towards the end of the play. "I say to myself- sometimes, Clov, you must be better than that if you want them to let you go - one day." (51) Apart from that self-insecurity, what seems to keep Clov in the shelter is, in Hamm's words, "The dialogue." (40) But although it may seem so, Hamm and Clov are not holding a dialogue; Hamm usually ignores Clov's reply, he thinks in terms of his own world, answering with sentences which do not correspond. CLOV "I'll leave you, I have things to do." HAMM "Do you remember when you came here?"(29) We may even suggest that Hamm's not-listening to Clov's statements *is* their dialogue, it keeps it alive, it is the cause of Clov's not leaving him. The fact that their dialogue is inexistent makes it possible for them to talk to each other. On the other hand, Clov impulsively answers in a pessimistic way, just to contradict Hamm. HAMM "Nature has forgotten us." CLOV "There is no more nature." But Clov's statements are not definitive. In response to Hamm's reply ("No more nature! You exaggerate."), he corrects himself "In the vicinity." (16), with the contradiction this implies.

Clov also lies to Hamm, in order to avoid any discussion. When he hands the black dog to Hamm (30), the blind man asks him "He his white, isn't he?", and his reply is "Nearly. " Clov does not want to cheat Hamm; in fact when Hamm asks him "What do you mean, nearly? Is he white or isn't he?", he answers "He isn't." Hamm does not know what colour the dog is, but he does not care (nor does Clov have any qualms about not telling the truth). Clov chooses the easiest way of answering Hamm's question, but he is not able to lie openly to him, because this could suggest that he is self-confident, precise, reliable, and consequently able to set up a dialogue, or at least that he could provoke a reaction.

When Hamm asks questions related to time "Have you not had enough?" (13) or "Do you not think this has gone on long enough?" (33), Clov answers "Yes!", and after a pause "Of what?", "What?" Clov has had enough of everything, whatever Hamm may mean in his dialectic speech; but the fact that he does not know what Hamm refers to denotes a strong lack of interest in Hamm's words. In doing so, Clov frustrates Hamm's dramatic performance.

Ruby Cohn claims:

> Clov is magnetised towards his kitchen, whereas Hamm tries to detain him. Nagg and Nell mirror such tension, Nagg trying to detain Nell, while they too repeat residually. For both *Endgame*'s couples, words are a weapon against time, but each blade is tempered to its own degree of repetition: Hamm most versatile, Clov more echoic, Nagg fainter and Nell faintest. (1979; 202)

In *Endgame* repetition of words and sentences, apart from being comical, underline the difference between the characters. Hamm and Clov, for example, repeat the same sentences even while their intentions differ. HAMM "Is Mother Pegg's light on?" CLOV "Light! How could anyone's light be on?" HAMM "Extinguished!" CLOV "Naturally it's extinguished. If it's not on, it's extinguished." HAMM "No, I meant Mother Pegg." (31) Bersani claims that "[t]he literal interpretations of speech kill its symbolic indeterminacy. With the sense of each utterance immediately exhausted by the response it evokes, language continuously rehearses its absorption into the final, unbroken "pause" or silence." (46)

The repetitions that link the couples' dialogues cannot be considered communicative, in that they are part of a monologue the characters are speaking. Beckett uses these repetitions to give the impression that the characters are speaking together, but they are not.

The dialogues of Nagg and Nell are "a travesty of communication" (Chevigny, 6). They try to talk, although they cannot see, nor hardly hear, each other anymore. Their discussion is an elegy of the past (a usual comment is "Ah yesterday!"), the April afternoon on Lake Como, their accident in the Ardennes, the sawdust which once was in the lid. When their speech is concerned with the present, Nagg usually has a request ("Do you want a bit?" (19) "Could you give me a scratch before you go?" 20), to which Nell at first answers, like Clov, negatively and aggressively. But then she asks for more information ("No. Of What?" "No. Where?"). When Nagg tries to recreate the joyful atmosphere of their past, by telling the story of the tailor (21-2), he fails. All that he is able to cause is a yearning for that time "You could see down to the bottom" is Nell's comment on the story, remembering the lake. Nagg and Nell do not speak either. If between Hamm and Clov the ruler is Hamm, between Nagg and Nell there is a sort of equality, and the powerful element seems to be Time (the past).

The audience is addressed quite directly by the characters on stage. Hamm and Clov are both aware of its presence, but they react differently. Hamm adds a second - acted - identity, that he has chosen himself, to his own (if he has one of his own, anyhow the audience will not experience it.) Hamm is conscious of the part he plays. Two of his speeches begin with the words "Me to play." (12, 44); he feels that he is being watched (45); he throws the whistle towards the auditorium and then covers his face with the handkerchief, refusing to interact with the people sitting in the theatre. (52) Clov notices the audience's presence through the telescope "I see . . . a multitude . . . in transports . . . of joy." (25), but he is not influenced by that presence either. He does not laugh.

The audience is watching a play which

> is aware of itself as a text performed in a theatre. It is sufficient to list the technical theatrical terms used in it in order to remark the rigor with which this effect is created: "farce," "auditorium," "aside," "soliloquy," "dialogue," "underplot," "exit." (Easthope, 66)

The spectators can interact with the characters on stage, or better *could*, but this dialogue fails because both parts are unable to influence the other; the audience cannot enter the world of the shelter, and the characters are not able to conform to something different from their own life.

So far, *Endgame* seems to be a drama of incommunication, a play in which the staticity of the plot should give importance to the dialogues, but fails. The speeches are pure monologues of (differently) troubled people.

There are, in *Endgame*, some scenes where tension is supposed to occur. The situations are the basis for a quarrel and, possibly, a change in the action, but these preliminaries are always frustrated. Clov does not pay attention to Hamm's problems, nor does Hamm himself.[79] To the news that there is no more pain-killer, Hamm reacts with an hysterical "What'll I do? What'll I do?", but Clov's indifference makes him stop and ask "What are you doing?" (46). A further example are Hamm's threats. "I'll give you nothing more to eat." But this does not alarm Clov, who answers "Then we'll die". Hamm replies "I'll give you just enough to keep you from dying. You'll be hungry all the time." And Clov says "Then we shan't die." (14) When Hamm's dramatic acting is ignored by Clov's indifference, Hamm does not know how to go on, and the suspense ends:

> HAMM: Do you know what's happened?
> CLOV: When? Where?
> HAMM: (*violently.*) When! What's happened! Use your head, can't you! What has happened?
> CLOV: What for Christ's sake does it matter?
> *He looks out of window.*
> HAMM: I don't know.
> *Pause. Clov turns towards Hamm.* (47-8)

We can see how the pauses and the differences in the tone of the voices (violent versus calm), are there to preclude the tension and, consequently, a real conflict.

The short dialogue between Hamm and Nagg (37-9), which ends with Nagg's curse, is another example of the failure to produce a climate of tension in the relationship between the characters of the play. The complete indifference which Hamm shows on hearing Nagg's words, is a sign of his egocentricity and of his not looking forward to anything anymore.

Also between Nagg and Nell there are some moments in which tension arises. When Nell criticises Nagg's laughing at Hamm's unhappiness: "One mustn't laugh at those things, Nagg. Why must you always laugh at them?", he answers "Not so loud!" (20), being afraid of the reaction Hamm might have if he heard their words, and not feeling ashamed because of the reproach Nell has made.

The audience's feeling about the dramatic tension in *Endgame* decreases as the performance proceeds. The only uncertainty in the plot (will Clov leave Hamm?) does not interest the spectator by the end of the play, it is inessential (and finally remains unresolved). At the beginning Clov's sentence "I'll leave you." keeps the audience in suspense because of it's straightness and cruelty, but the numerous repetitions progressively weaken its strength. The fact that Hamm and Clov are aware of someone sitting in front of them, can be disagreeable for the audience, which is exposed to the characters' (and to

Beckett's) affection and therefore is directly taking part in the play. This tension fades only at the end of *Endgame*, when Clov disappears and Hamm rejects any further communication by covering his face with the handkerchief. But the audience is left with another doubt. Hamm's last words are "Since that's the way we're playing it . . . let's play it that way . . . and speak no more about it . . . " (52). Hamm himself, the on-stage author of *Endgame*, cannot react to the inevitable ending, the situation slips out of his hands, he is annihilated. The audience, in this last dramatic moment, joins him in that silent and motionless world.

Chevigny claims:

> [t]he characters share the scepticism of the author and strikingly anticipate that of the audience by continually undercutting whatever might have been convincing, belying what seemed authentic, exploding all behaviour as self-conscious performance. (9)

Hamm and Clov deny any discussion which could imply a meaning. Any exchange of opinion is hinted at, but is then skilfully avoided. After having heard the ringing of the alarm-clock, Clov asks "Did you hear it?", and Hamm answers "Vaguely." CLOV "The end is terrific." HAMM "I prefer the middle."[80] Here there could be communication (although limited to a banal controversy), but Hamm, after a pause, takes the dialogue back to what has by now become for the audience the meaningless normality of repetition "Is it not time for my pain-killer?" Clov answers angrily "No!", and then comes back to normality, too "I'll leave you." (34)

Endgame is not a traditional drama, there is not a rise or a fall in the action, because, as Goldman claims "all is fallen at the play's opening." (38) So, the play moves towards a loss of all motion and being.[81] *Act without Words*, which follows *Endgame* in the Faber edition, is a sort of summing up; at the end the man does not react to the whistle, he lies on the floor, he does not move and looks at his hands. But for the audience the tension does not fall. This situation of immobility is not caused by the solving of the troubles in the plot; on the contrary, the problems overwhelm the characters and, consequently, the audience itself. Beckett draws the curtain without really ending the play, leaving the spectators, who are a part of it, with a feeling of emptiness. The audience is conscious of having had a part in *Endgame*, but does not understand which one; it asks itself what it should have done during the performance, and what it should do now. Beckett's message of incommunicability reaches the spectator only at the end, when the audience realises that "the only alternative to that absurdity is action" (Schlueter, 62), but does not know what to do. This is the final and permanent tension.

Beckett transfers the quest for self-realisation from a setting where monologues are held to one where there is (some kind of) dialogue. But we have seen that the dialogue is simply the sum of different monologues. Notice that "[f]or the Beckettian speaker, monologue is an experience of self-alienation rather than self-expression" (Bersani, 50). Why has Beckett thus applied a structure which only seems to contain dialogues? There are at least three answers: the first one is that Beckett wants to show that dialogue is not possible and is useless, that when persons try to interact they fail because each one speaks, using his personal vocabulary, about what he is interested in, and does not listen to - or understand - the other.[82]

The second one is that Hamm and Clov speak together because they depend on each other. Beckett describes the utilitarian aspect of dialogue as bestial (If I leave him / If he leaves me, I will die). Notice that if Clov would leave Hamm, speech would not continue, but this never happens. Like in *The Unnamable* words cannot stop, they have to go on.

The third answer is that inadequate dialogue is useful to demonstrate all the ties which bind human beings to the unnamable's "there" and which are not able to avoid the quest for "here".

Endgame is so powerful because its audience feels these aspects although there is no action or dialogue. In fact, it may be precisely because there is no action or dialogue that the effect upon the audience is all the more powerful. Beckett in a letter to Alan Schneider writes: "Hamm as stated, and Clov as stated, together as stated, nec tecum nec sine te, in such a place, and in such a world, that's all I can manage, more than I could." (*Disjecta*, 109) Nothing is present and nothing is absent. Beckett cannot add any theoretical explanation to his play because on his way to "here" there is also the destruction of every explanation. He seeks the void from which self-realisation stems. With *Endgame*, a collection of different kinds of emptiness, this goal is at hand. The audience understands it (each one in his personal way) and is both amazed and afraid of going that way. The final and lasting tension is a feeling of committed search into those things that all human beings have to look for if they want to be worthy of that name.

CONCLUSION

> D. – Why is he obliged to paint?
> B. – I don't know.
> (*Three Dialogues*, 142)

As already stated, Deirdre Bair in her *Biography* writes that "[i]t [*The Unnamable*] is one of his [Beckett's] two favourite works and like the other, *Endgame*, it is one which gives him enormous personal satisfaction." (425) It is from these two works that I have drawn the conclusions that make possible a more optimistic view of Samuel Beckett's poetry. The fact that they were Beckett's favourite works shows that in them he came closest to what he wanted to express, to the voice of the Muse, to the *unknown*.

This dissertation has tried to clarify some aspects correlated with Beckett's quest for the source from which his work has sprung. I have analysed how Beckett has carried out his research, the hindrances he has had to cope with, the results he has achieved.

In Part I, I tried to extrapolate from other sources some important aspects of Beckett's unexpressed theory of writing. I considered Plato and his idea that representation (by means of words) only slightly hints at real objects. With the help of *Ion*, I have concluded that Beckett's *unknown* is not a product of rationality, but transcends it. In Part I, Chapter 2, I analysed Beckett's work with the help of religious texts. After having considered some mechanisms described in the *Bhagavad-Gita*, I have concluded that Beckett's interest is for rationality, but his mind is inadequate to explain his spiritual part. With the help of medieval mystics, I have then analysed this tension and its results.

In Part II, I have concentrated on Beckett's writing process, on the levels on which the *unknown* produces a result. I have considered how the Irish writer composes his works and which are (some of) the literary sources that have helped him to develop his way of expressing the *unknown*. In the first chapter, by applying some elements of Dante's view of poetry, I considered the two levels that can be found in Beckett's work: the literal one, which copes with the destruction of traditional rules, and the allegorical one, which hints at the spiritual part. To enrich this view, I have added the comparison Beckett - Petrarch, showing how they both see that language cannot fully describe what they need to say. I have then considered two episodes taken from the *Commedia* in order to draw some parallelisms with the trilogy. In Part II, Chapter 2, I considered Gianbattista Vico's way of conceiving history (the distinction between "filosofia" and " filologia"); the three ages in which he divides the development of human society; his theories on language, poetry and myth; and finally the relationship between human beings and history. Vico's ideas helped us to consider Beckett's trilogy in relation to a division of human society into ages: Worm, the still unborn who does not exist; Molloy, the animistic product of nature; Moran, the product of society; Malone, the end of life; and the unnamable, the limbo inhabitant. They are all chained one to each other in a similar way to that described by Vico in his "teoria dei corsi e ricorsi storici".

In Part III, in order to look for a practical application of the theoretical results achieved in Part I and Part II, I concentrated on Beckett's trilogy of novels. I considered the structure of the decreasing movement contained in it. I analysed Molloy's - apparently chaotic - circular movements (physical, mental and in language); Moran's difficulty in understanding spirituality and his gradual loss of instinct and rationality; Malone's being resigned to the immortality of the tension which has immobilised him and which has arisen from the confrontations of his rationality with his spirituality; and finally the unnamable's standstill. The unnamable is already detached from instinct, rationality, language, but is not yet absorbed by the force he recognises as being the only one which absorbs all his interest. In Part III, Chapter 2, I have considered how the tension, still unresolved at

Conclusion

the end of the trilogy, has been developed in Beckett's plays. In the first part of the chapter we have seen how his plays contain only a starting point for the audience; how they do not present a particular theme but hint at a whole by describing a way of trying to realise it. The play I have taken into consideration in the second part of Chapter 2 is *Endgame*. I have tried to show how Hamm, Clov, Nagg and Nell are unable to subvert the immobile frustration we are presented with at the end of the trilogy. We have seen how Beckett uses different monologues in order to give us the impression of the presence of a dialogue. His aim is to show the inefficiency and the utilitarian aspect of dialogue. Beckett, in his quest for the unnamable's "here", tries to stigmatize all the ties that bind him "there".

To *approach* a solution is the greatest success of Beckett's writing and makes him one of the greatest writers of the 20th century. He does not propose particular solutions, but he proposes hope for those who need to search for an all-embracing answer. Beckett is a great writer in that he is receptive to a cosmic and universal matter, but he is also able to transfer this to his historical period and mask it with frustrating daily experiences; he is capable of describing the human essence considered in its historical conduct and take it back to its eternal and emblematic significance.

Niklaus Gessner in his *Die Unzulänglichkeit der Sprache* writes that: "es ist Beckett gelungen, den Untergang des sprachlichen Ausdruckes sprachlich auszudrücken und in einem Werk der Literatur das Ende der Literatur nicht bloss anzukündigen, sondern zu gestalten." (74) Gessner underlines Beckett's greatness: Beckett does not *describe* the end of literature but *demonstrates* it. Beckett's careful writings are near to their source, they do not need to describe the force that has created them because source and writings are so close to each other that they often are confused. The reader or the audience feel the presence of the god of poetry and Beckett's proximity to him, and are fascinated. Ancient myths tried to describe with images an unsayable reality, Beckett, in his work, tries to picture an unsayable mystery. Beckett's greatest achievement is being able to communicate, thanks to his endless quest, his hope of discovering the *unknown*, of accomplishing a rational self-realisation, of immersing himself in Silence.

BIBLIOGRAPHY

Primary Sources

Beckett, Samuel. *The Complete Dramatic Works*. London: Faber and Faber, 1986.

---. "Dante . . . Bruno . Vico . . Joyce." 1929. *Disjecta*. Ed. Ruby Cohn. London: John Calder, 1983. 19-33.

---. *Disjecta. Miscellaneous Writings and a Dramatic Fragment*. Ed. Ruby Cohn. London: John Calder, 1983.

---. *Dream of Fair to Middling Women*. New York: Arcade Publishing, 1992.

---. *Eleutheria*. Paris: Les Editions de Minuit, 1995.

---. *Endgame*. 1958. London: Faber and Faber, 1964.

---. *Endgame, with a Revised Text*. Ed. S.E. Gontarsky. London: Faber and Faber, 1992.

---. *First Love*. 1946. London: John Calder, 1973.

---. *How It Is*. London: John Calder, 1964.

---. *Lessness*. London: Calder & Boyards, 1970.

---. "Lettre à Georges Duthuit à propos de Bram van Velde". *Bram van Velde. 1895-1981. Rétrospective du centenaire*. Ed. Rainer Michael Mason. Genève: Musée Rath, 1996. 45-48.

---. *Malone Dies*. 1956. *The Beckett Trilogy*. London: Picador, 1979. 163-264.

---. *Mercier and Camier*. 1970. London: Picador, 1988.

---. *Molloy*. 1955. *The Beckett Trilogy*. London: Picador, 1979. 7-162.

---. *More Pricks Than Kicks*. 1934. London: John Calder, 1966.

---. *Murphy*. 1938. London: Picador, 1973.

---. "On Endgame." *Disjecta*. Ed. Ruby Cohn. London: John Calder, 1983. 106-110.

---. *Proust*. 1930. London: Calder & Boyards, 1965.

---. "Text". *The European Caravan*. Ed. Samuel Putnam. New York: 1931. 478-80.

---. "Three Dialogues." 1949. *Disjecta*. Ed. Ruby Cohn. London: John Calder, 1983. 138-145.

---. *The Unnamable*. 1959. *The Beckett Trilogy*. London: Picador, 1979. 265-382.

---. *Warten auf Godot/ En attendant Godot/ Waiting for Godot*. 1952 Frankfurt am Main: Suhrkamp, 1971.

---. *Waiting for Godot, with a Revised Text*. Ed. Dougald Mcmillan and James Knowlson. London: Faber and Faber, 1993.

---. *Watt.* 1953. London: John Calder, 1976.

---. *Worstward Ho.* London: John Calder, 1983.

Secondary Sources

Acheson, James. "Chess with the audience: Samuel Beckett's *Endgame*." *Critical Quarterly*. 22 (Summer 1980): 33-46.

Admussen, Richard. *The Samuel Beckett Manuscripts. A Study*. London: George Prior, 1979.

Adorno, Theodor W. "Trying to Understand *Endgame*". *Modern Critical Views: Samuel Beckett*. Ed. Harold Bloom. New York: Chelsea House, 1985. 51-81.

Alighieri, Dante. "Epistola XIII to Cangrande della Scala." *La Letteratura Italiana. Storia e Testi*. Ed. Giorgio Brugnoli et al. 82 vols. Milano / Napoli: Ricciardi, 1979. 5 (Tomo 2): 598-643.

---. *Inferno*. Vol. 1 of *La Divina Commedia*. Ed. Natalino Sapegno. 3 vols. Firenze: La Nuova Italia, 1955.

---. *Purgatorio*. Vol. 2 of *La Divina Commedia*. Ed. Natalino Sapegno. 3 vols. Firenze: La Nuova Italia, 1955.

---. *Paradiso*. Vol. 3 of *La Divina Commedia*. Ed. Natalino Sapegno. 3 vols. Firenze: La Nuova Italia, 1955.

---. *The Divine Comedy*. Trans. Henry Cary. London: Heron Books, 1970.

Arnheim, Rudolf. *Entropy and Art. An Essay on Disorder and Order*. Berkeley: University of California, 1971.

Bair, Deirdre. *Samuel Beckett. A Biography*. 1978. London: Vintage, 1990.

Bersani, Leo. *The Culture of Redemption*. Cambridge and London: Harward University, 1990.

Bersani, Leo and Ulysse Dutoit. *Arts of Impoverishment. Beckett, Rothko, Resnais*. London: Harvard University, 1993.

Bloom, Harold. *A Map of Misreading*. Oxford: Oxford University, 1980.

---. *Modern Critical Views: Samuel Beckett*. New York: Chelsea House, 1985. 51-81.

---. *Samuel Beckett*. New Haven: Chelsea House, 1985.

Brater, Enoch, ed. *Around the Absurd*. Ann Arbor: University of Michigan, 1990.

Bryden, Mary. "Beckett and the Three Dantean Smiles." *Journal of Beckett Studies*. Vol. 4 N° 2 (1995): 29-33.

Budick, Sanford and Wolfgang Iser. "Introduction." *Languages of the Unsayable*. Eds. Sanford Budick and Wolfgang Iser. New York: Columbia University, 1989. xi-xxi.

Busi, Frederick. *The Transformation of Godot*. Lexington: Kentucky University, 1980.

Cattanei, Giovanni. *Samuel Beckett*. Firenze: La Nuova Italia, 1980.

Chambers, Ross. "An Approach to *Endgame*." *Twentieth Century Interpretations of Endgame*. Ed. Bell Gale Chevigny. Englewood Cliffs: Prentice-Hall, 1969. 71-81.

Chevigny, Bell Gale. "Introduction." *Twentieth Century Interpretations of Endgame.* Ed. Bell Gale Chevigny. Englewood Cliffs: Prentice-Hall, 1969. 1-13.

Cioran, Emile Michel. "Encounter With Beckett." *Samuel Beckett: The Critical Heritage* Eds. Lawrence Graver and Raymond Federman. London: Routledge and Kegan Paul, 1979. 334-339.

Cognet, Louis. *Introduction aux mystiques rhéno-flamands.* Paris: Desclée, 1968.

Cohn, Ruby. *Back to Beckett.* Princeton: University Press, 1973.

---, ed. *Beckett: Waiting for Godot. A Casebook.* London: Macmillan, 1987.

---. *From Desire to Godot.* Berkley: University of California, 1987.

---. *Just Play: Beckett's Theater.* Princeton: University Press, 1980.

---. "Words Working Overtime: Endgame and No Man's Land." *Yearbook of English Studies.* 9 (1979): 188-203.

D'Aubarède, Gabriel. 1961. "Interview With Beckett." *Samuel Beckett: The Critical Heritage* Eds. Lawrence Graver and Raymond Federman. London: Routledge and Kegan Paul, 1979. 215-7

Descartes, René. *Discours de la méthode.* 1637. *Œuvres et lettres.* Ed. André Bridoux. Paris: Gallimard, 1953. 123-167.

Driver, Tom. 1961. "Interview with Samuel Beckett." *Samuel Beckett: The Critical Heritage* Eds. Lawrence Graver and Raymond

Federman. London: Routledge and Kegan Paul, 1979. 217-223.

Duckworth, Colin. *Angels of Darkness: Dramatic Effect in Samuel Beckett with Special Reference to Eugène Ionesco*. London: George Allen & Unwin Ltd, 1972.

Easthope, Anthony. "Hamm, Clov, and Dramatic Method in *Endgame*." *Twentieth Century Interpretations of Endgame*. Ed. Bell Gale Chevigny. Englewood Cliffs: Prentice-Hall, 1969. 61-70.

Esslin, Martin. *An Anathomy of Drama*. London: Temple Smith, 1976.

---. "Samuel Beckett: The Search for the Self." *Twentieth Century Interpretations of Endgame*. Ed. Bell Gale Chevigny. Englewood Cliffs: Prentice-Hall, 1969. 22-32.

---. *Théatre de l'Absurde*. Paris: Buchet / Chastel, 1977.

Fabietti, Renato. *La filosofia nell'epoca moderna e le rivoluzioni scientifica, religiosa e politica*. Vol. 2 of *Filosofie e società*. 3 vols. Bologna: Zanichelli, 1985.

Fitch, Brian T. *Dimensions, structures, et textualité, dans la trilogie romanesque de Beckett*. Paris: Minard, 1977.

Fletcher, Beryl, et al. *A Student's Guide to the Plays of Samuel Beckett*. London: Faber and Faber, 1978.

Fletcher, John. *Beckett: His Works and His Critics*. Berkley: University of California, 1970.

Friedrich, Hugo. *Die Struktur der modernen Lyrik*. Hamburg:

Rowohlt, 1956.

Gessner, Niklaus. *Die Unzulänglichkeit der Sprache*. Zürich: Juris Verlag, 1957.

Goldman, Richard M. "*Endgame* and its Scorekeepers." *Twentieth Century Interpretations of Endgame*. Ed. Bell Gale Chevigny. Englewood Cliffs: Prentice-Hall, 1969. 33-39.

Graver, Lawrence and Raymond Federman, eds. *Samuel Beckett: The Critical Heritage*. London: Routledge and Kegan Paul, 1979.

Gussow, Mel. "Interview with Samuel Beckett". *New York Times* 31. Dec. 1989: Arts and Leisure Section, 3.

Hildesheimer, Wolfgang. "Über das absurde Theater." 1960. *Gesammelte Werke in sieben Bänder*. 7 vols. Frankfurt am Main: Suhrkamp, 1991. 7: 13-26.

Hughes, Peter. "From Allusion to Implosion. Vico. Michelet. Joyce, Beckett." *Vico and Joyce*. Ed. Verene, Donald Phillip. New York: State University, 1987. 83-99.

Hunkeler, Thomas. *Echos de l'ego dans l'oeuvre de Samuel Beckett*. Paris: L'Harmattan, 1997.

Kenner, Hugh. *Samuel Beckett. A Critical Study*. Berkley: University of California, 1968.

Knowlson, James. *Damned to Fame. The Life of Samuel Beckett*. London: Bloomsbury, 1996.

Bibliography: Secondary Sources

Lake, Carlton, ed. *No Symbols Where None Intended. A Catalogue of Books, Manuscripts, and Other Material Relating to Samuel Beckett in the Collections of the Humanities Research Center.* Austin: University of Texas, 1984.

Lossky, Vladimir. *Théologie négative et connaissance de Dieu chez Maître Eckhart.* Paris: J. Vain, 1973.

Mason, Rainer Michael, ed. *Bram van Velde. 1895-1981. Rétrospective du centenaire.* Genève: Musée Rath, 1996.

Petrarca, Francesco. *Secretum.* 1343. *La Letteratura Italiana. Storia e Testi.* Ed. Guido Martellotti et al. 82 vols. Milano / Napoli: Ricciardi, 1979. 7: 22-215.

Pilling, John and Mary Bryden, eds. *The Ideal Core of the Onion.* Reading: Beckett International Foundation, 1992.

Plato. "Epistle VII." *Plato in Twelve Volumes.* Trans. R. G. Bury. London: William Heinemann, 1975. 9: 477-565.

---. "Ion." *Plato in Twelve Volumes.* Trans. W. R. M. Lamb. London: William Heinemann, 1975. 8: 403-447.

---. "Phaedrus." *Plato in Twelve Volumes.* Trans. Harold North Fowler. London: William Heinemann, 1977. 1: 413-579.

Prabhupada, Bhaktivedanta, ed. *Bhagavad-Gita, As It Is.* Borehamwood / Los Angeles: Bhaktivedanta Book Trust, 1986.

---. "Setting the Scene." *Bhagavad-Gita, As It Is.* Borehamwood / Los Angeles: Bhaktivedanta Book Trust, 1986. xiii-xv.

Reale, Giovanni and Dario Antiseri. *Il pensiero occidentale dalle origini ad oggi*. 3 vols. Brescia: La Scuola, 1987.

Reale, Giovanni. *Storia della filosofia antica*. 9th edition. 5 vols. Milano: Vita e Pensiero, 1992.

Robinson, Michael. "From Purgatory to Inferno: Beckett and Dante Revisited". *Journal of Beckett Studies*. N° 5 (Autumn 1979): 69-82.

Rossi, Paolo. "Introduzione". *La Scienza Nuova*. 1744. Ed. Paolo Rossi. Milano: Rizzoli, 1977. 5-59.

Said, Edward W. *Beginnings*. New York: Basic Books, 1975.

Saint Augustine, Aurelius. *Confessionum. Libri Tredecim*. Vol 1 of *Opere di Sant'Agostino. Edizione latino-italiana*. Eds. Michele Pellegrino and Carlo Carena. Roma: Città Nuova, 1965.

Schlueter, June. *Metafictional Characters in Modern Drama*. New York: Columbia University, 1977.

Schneider, Alan. "Waiting for Beckett: A Personal Chronical." *Twentieth Century Interpretations of Endgame*. Ed. Bell Gale Chevigny. Englewood Cliffs: Prentice-Hall, 1969. 14-21.

Shenker, Israel. 1956. "An Interview with Samuel Beckett." *Samuel Beckett: The Critical Heritage* Eds. Lawrence Graver and Raymond Federman. London: Routledge and Kegan Paul, 1979. 146-9.

Sherzer, Dina. *Structure de la Trilogie de Beckett*. The Hague-Paris: Mouton, 1976.

Simoni, Silvano. "Introduzione all'*Imitazione di Cristo.*" *Mistici del XIV secolo.* Torino: Unione tipografica / Editrice Torinese, 1972. 9-31.

Tagliaferri, Aldo. *Beckett e l'iperdeterminazione letteraria.* Milano: Feltrinelli, 1979.

Thomas A Kempis. *Of the Imitation of Christ.* Trans. omitted. London: Rivingtons, 1874.

Vico, Giambattista. *De antiquissima Italorum sapientia ex linguae latinae originibus eruenda.* 1710. *Opere filosofiche.* Ed. Paolo Cristofolini. Firenze: Sansoni, 1971. 55-131.

---. *De nostri temporis studiorum ratione.* 1708. *Opere filosofiche.* Ed. Paolo Cristofolini. Firenze: Sansoni, 1971. 787-857.

---. *La Scienza Nuova.* 1744. Ed. Paolo Rossi. Milano: Rizzoli, 1977.

Wilkins, Ernest Hatch. *Life of Petrarch.* Chicago and London: University of Chicago, 1961.

Wolosky, Shira. "Samuel Beckett's Figural Evasion." *Languages of the Unsayable.* Eds. Sanford Budick and Wolfgang Iser. New York: Columbia University, 1989. 163-85.

About the Author

The first part of Andreas Barella's education has been humanistic. He studied English literature and linguistics and Italian literature and linguistics at Zürich University (1988-1994). From 1994 to 1998 he wrote a Ph.D. for Zürich University on philosophical influences in the work of Samuel Beckett. In 1999 he published his first book *A Language of the Unknown. Influence and Composition in the Work of Samuel Beckett*.

The second part of his education – the experiential part – consists of the *Scuola di psicoterapia integrata* directed in Lugano by Dr. Med. Romano Daguet (1999-2002), and the Advanced Training of the *School of Gestalt and Experiential Teaching* of San Francisco, directed by Paul Rebillot (Frankfurt Am Main, 2003-2005).

Between 2003 and 2010 he has assisted Paul Rebillot at his *School of Gestalt and Experiential Teaching* (European Branch). He leads classes, workshops and supervisions in several psychotherapy schools and post-doc institutions. He has written three books and edited the Italian version of Paul Rebillot's *The Hero's Journey*.

Since 2003 he helps people in his office in Mendrisio (Switzerland) and coaches senior managers and their teams around the world. He leads workshops in Switzerland, Italy, France, Germany, Austria, and the US. He works in collaboration with many institutions, e.g. Corsi per Adulti of the Dipartimento dell'educazione della cultura e dello sport del Canton Ticino (DECS), Organizzazione Sociopsichiatrica Cantonale (OSC), Alta Scuola Pedagogica in Locarno (ASP), Istituto Universitario Federale per la Formazione Professionale in Lugano (IUFFP), Divisione della formazione professionale del DECS, Dipartimento della Sanità e della

Socialità del Canton Ticino (DSS), WWF Switzerland, Alpen-Initiative, OTAF Foundation Lugano, Centro di studi naturali e prevenzione Alchemilla in Balerna, Swiss Radio and Television Broadcasting Corporation (RSI), Associazione Ticinese Famiglie Affidatarie (ATFA), the newspaper la Regione.

Info and contacts:
www.andreasbarella.com
info@andreasbarella.com

PUBLISHING HISTORY

The first edition of this book has been published in Zürich (Switzerland) in 1999 and has been presented to the Faculty of Arts of the University of Zürich for the degree of Doctor of Philosophy by Andreas Barella of Muggio – Ticino, and accepted on the Recommendation of Professor PETER HUGHES, Ph.D.

[1] Notice how Beckett underlines this dichotomy again in a late work: "How almost true [the words] sometimes almost ring! How wanting in inanity!" (*Worstward Ho*, 21). Words are an illusion, but they seem true and real.

[2] Beckett is aware of that condition and his works are carefully constructed to show it. Nevertheless, he is not able to find a solution. Notice also that Beckett's subjects are not the human characters of his plays and novels, but this *something else* that the Irish writer does not understand himself.

[3] James Knowlson describes how Beckett compiled notebooks with quotes taken from several authors with the idea of using them in his works. Cf., for example, page 109: "He copied out dozens of passages, mostly verbatim, from the text [St. Augustine's *Confessions*]. [...] A private notebook of Beckett gives chapter and verse to his many borrowings from St Augustine. It is not that he plagiarises. He makes no attempt to hide what he is doing. Anyone familiar with St Augustine's book would recognise the passages involved. He merely uses the quotations to underline the contrasting demands of flesh and spirit and to add levels of philosophical allusion for his own delight and for the pleasure or amusement of the reader."

[4] My choices are not definitive nor exhaustive, and they may be enriched by additional evidence.

[5] Beckett's "chaos" and "mess" are definitions which imply confusion and disorder and thus cannot be considered exhaustive.

[6] I use the expressions 'soul', and further on, 'spiritual part of a man' in their wider sense. I have considered spiritual everything which is not rationally explicable.

[7] This last question, "What is Beckett writing about?" is the most difficult one. Provisionally, I will call this mysterious engine of Beckett's creativity TRUTH. I have chosen a term often used in connection with religion because the force that pushes Beckett to write has to be considered the most important component of his

being a poet; the primigenial means of research; the need to know and understand.

[8] Beckett's works cannot be considered comical, or at least not purely comical. His characters' behaviour is a mixture of funny and dramatic elements. Some of these recurrent structures of Beckett's works will be discussed in Part III. Here I am dealing with the stylistic choices applied in a specific work.

[9] Why and how Beckett actually does this is the topic of Part III.

[10] The fact of not knowing what Truth is is not important if the reader feels it inside and if it strives to become clear: "such words [about justice and beauty and goodness] should be considered the speaker's own legitimate offspring" (*Phaedrus*, 573-5).

[11] Even though another part of his being denies it.

[12] The period of Beckett's life in which this duty is most felt, is that between the writing of *Molloy* and the composition of *Endgame*. The works included in that period are: *Molloy* (written in 1948), *Malone meurt* (1948), *En attendant Godot* (1948-9), the translation of Suzanne's *F* (1948-9?); *Three Dialogues with Georges Duthuit* (1949); *L'innomable* (1950); and *Fin de partie* together with *Act sans paroles I*. The works written before that stretch of time are too experimental (Beckett is still trying to understand the voice), while the ones written after are either too pondered and too specific, or a variation-spreading out of an already mentioned theme. An example is the "Willie-Winnie Notes", used for the creation of *Happy Days*. These notes attack religious observance in Ireland, the Catholic Church and its priests; they condemn both the church's and the British government's domination of the Irish people. They are an example of Beckett's more conscious creation process. Beckett is still possessed by the Muse, but he is accustomed to her presence and can mix it with his thoughts. Notice that Beckett himself claimed in 1956 that he had written all his best works between 1946 and 1950 (quoted in Tagliaferri, 12). Knowlson in his chapter "A Frenzy of Writing, 1946-53" describes this period as follows:

"These three novels [*Molloy, Malone Dies, The Unnamable*], along with *En attendant Godot*, are the finest pieces of writing to emerge from this extraordinary fertile [...] period. They are almost certainly the most enduring works that Beckett wrote." (371)

[13] When dealing with Beckett's plays, another factor has to be considered i.e. the impulsive interpretation due to the abundance of symbols. The 1953 first "prison-production" of Godot in Lüttringhausen, near Wuppertal in Germany, and the several subsequent prison performances of *Waiting for Godot* are clear examples: the prisoners did not find the play difficult at all, each of them giving a particular interpretation of what had happened on stage.

[14] Beckett, quoted in Duckworth, claims that Christianity is "a mythology with which I am perfectly familiar. So naturally I use it." (18)

[15] Aldo Tagliaferri in his *Beckett e l'iperdeterminazione letteraria*, quotes and comments a passage from the *Brhadaranyaka Upanisad* in order to discuss Beckett's development of ancient myths. We will use the *Bhagavad-Gita* in order to underline the presence of a similar force in Beckett and in Krishna's words to Arjuna.

[16] Notice that the choice is not between good and bad, but between righteous (term which cannot imply proudness on the side of the performer of the action) and negligent.

[17] Of course the bohemiène aspect of this way of living has to be considered too.

[18] But notice that in a letter to Aldo Tagliaferri (19.12.1987, in possession of the Beckett Archive in Reading, MS 4090) to Tagliaferri's statement: "Charles Juliet deals briefly with the interest you once took in great western mystics (Saint Jean de la Croix, Maître Eckhart, Ruusbroek)", Beckett writes: "No memory of such mention. Juliet unreliable source. No particular interest in mysticism that I can recall."

[19] Notice the similarity with the already considered Platonic

invitation to interiority.

[20] To these two elements we must add Beckett's conscious and rational refusal to recognise his intuition as being essential, and his need to show that any attempt to entrap him in whatever theory is limiting.

[21] Notice that Molloy claims that he loves that method: "What I liked in anthropology was its inexhaustible faculty of negation, its relentless definition of man, as though he were no better than God, <u>in terms of what he is not</u>." (38, emphasis added)

[22] On the contrary, Spinoza claims that every deduction stems from a metaphysical and logical deduction, cf. Part III, the chapter on the unnamable.

[23] For a more detailed description of the sermons in which that concept is applied cf. Lossky, 1973.

[24] Notice that in this chapter I will only consider those aspects of the trilogy mentioned in the *Imitatione Christi*. For a detailed analysis of Molloy, Moran, Malone and the unnamable, cf. Part III.

[25] I would like to underline that what I am suggesting here is that Thomas A Kempis's description of a mystic way of life is similar to the way Beckett's characters operate in their world, and not that Molloy, Moran, Malone, the unnamable and Beckett himself are directly interested in mysticism.

[26] Of course it is a relative freedom because the reader is made aware of the severe conditions of Hell. Notice the difference between Krishna, who makes the difference between righteous and negligent (cf. Part 1, the chapter on the *Bhagavad-Gita*), and Dante, who divides people between good and evil.

[27] The controversy tragedy-comedy in Beckett's drama will be considered in Part III, Ch. 2.

[28] For excerpts from the translation of the *Divina Commedia*, I refer to Henry Cary, Heron Books, 1970.

[29] "Such is this steep ascent, / That it is ever difficult at first, / But more a man proceeds, less evil grows. / When pleasant it shall

seem to thee, so much / That upward going shall be easy to thee / As in a vessel to go down the tide, / Then of this path thou wilt have reach'd the end. / There hope to rest thee from thy toil. No more / I answer, and thus far for certain know." / As he his words had spoken, near to us / A voice there sounded: "Yet ye first perchance / May to repose you constraint be led." (164)

[30] Notice Dante's description of how Sordello is sitting: "Venimmo a lei: o anima lombarda, / come ti stavi altera e disdegnosa / e nel muover delli occhi onesta e tarda! / Ella non ci dicea alcuna cosa, / ma lasciavane gir, solo sguardando / a guisa di leon quando si posa." (*Purgatorio*, vi, 61-66) Malone will use Dante's episode in order to describe one of the participants of Lady Pedal's excursion: "the youth had thrown himself down in the shade of a rock, like Sordello, but less noble, for Sordello resembled a lion at rest" (262). Notice how Malone, like Molloy before, mingles Belacqua and Sordello: Dante does not say that Sordello sits in the shade of a rock. Malone confuses him with Belacqua sitting "all'ombra dietro al sasso" (*Purg.*, iv, 105). When Sordello happens to know that Virgil stems out of his same town (i.e. Mantova), he stands up from where he was lying still and apart from the other souls, and hugs Virgil (*Purg.*, vi, 67-75). Dante comments on this episode by saying that Sordello embraces Virgil only because of their common origin, and that such an episode would be impossible in the Italy of his present time because on earth everybody considers only the possibility of gaining money and political power. Here, again, we have an example of Beckett's lessening and parodying a strongly claimed idea: Dante's polemics about the decadence of Italian political life is parodied by Beckett in Lady Pedal's organising the excursion; Dante's political passion becomes Lady Pedal's devotion "for doing good and bringing a little happiness into the lives of these less fortunate than herself" (*Malone Dies*, 257). Politics become a comical benefaction and corruption becomes "an interest in the inmates of Saint John of God's" (257).

[31] "At sound thereof each turn'd; and on the left / A huge stone

we beheld, of which nor I / Not he before was ware. Thither we drew; / And there were some, who in the shady place / Behind the rock were standing, as a man / Through idleness might stand. Among them one, / Who seem'd to be much wearied, sat him down, / And with his arms did fold his knees about, / Holding his face between them downward bent" (164).

[32] In Hell there is only one smile and it is Virgil's, when the four great souls of the joyful limbo ("la bella scola" (the bright school): Homer, Horace, Ovid and Lucan) welcome Dante among them (*Inf.*, iv, 94-102). But the joyful limbo is extremely different from the Ante-Purgatory because Dante was forced to include the former in his *Comedy* because of the classical description of the underworld (he certainly knew Homer's *Odyssey* and Virgil's *Aeneid*). The Ante-Purgatory has no forebear in former works.

In Paradise, Beatrice often smiles at Dante's human fragility; her smile is always a mixture of affection and of pity.

[33] "[...] if prayer do not aid me first, / That riseth up from heart which lives in grace." (165)

[34] In fact, a sleeping Dante will be brought up to Purgatory's doors by Santa Lucia; Dante does not need to walk through the Ante-Purgatory. Molloy and Moran, lacking Dante's faith, have to ramble through Ballybaba.

[35] Cf. Beckett's 1931 poem "Text" which is well aware of Canto III of Dante's Hell.

[36] "Here sighs, with lamentations and loud moans, / Resounded through the air pierced by no star, / That e'en I wept at entering. Various tongues, / Horrible languages, outcries of woe, / Accents of anger, voices deep and hoarse, / With hands together smote that swell'd the sounds, / Made up a tumult, that for ever whirls / Round through that air with solid darkness stain'd, / Like to the sand that in the whirlwind flies." (10)

[37] "I then, with error yet encompast, cried: / "O master! what is this I hear? what race / Are these, who seem so overcome with woe?" / He thus to me: "This miserable fate / Suffer the wretched

souls of those, who lived / Without or praise or blame, with that ill band / Of angels mix'd, who nor rebellious proved, / Nor yet were true to God, but for themselves / Were only. From his bounds Heaven drove them forth, / Not to impair his lustre; nor the depth / Of Hell receives them, lest the accursed tribe / Should glory thence with exultation vain." / I then: "Master! what doth aggrieve them thus, / That they lament so loud?" He straight replied: / "That will I tell thee briefly. These of death / No hope may entertain: and their blind life / So meanly passes, that all other lots / They envy. Fame of them the world hath none, / Nor suffers; Mercy and Justice scorn them both. / Speak not of them, but look, and pass them by." (10-1)

[38] Remember the already quoted letter to Georges Duthuit: "Pour ma part, c'est le *gran rifiuto* qui m'intéresse, non pas les héroïques tortillements auxquels nous devons une chose si belle." (Mason, 46) Beckett knew and remembered this passage.

[39] "And I, who straightway look'd, beheld a flag, / Which whirling ran around so rapidly, / That it no pause obtain'd: and following came / Such a long train of spirits, I should ne'er / Have thought that death so many had despoil'd. / When some of these I recognised, I saw / And knew the shade of him, who to base fear / Yielding, abjured his high estate. Forthwith / I understood, for certain, this the tribe / Of those ill spirits both to God displeasing / And to His foes. These wretches, who ne'er lived, / Went on in nakedness, and sorely stung / By wasps and hornets, which bedew'd their cheeks / With blood, that, mix'd with tears, dropp'd to their feet, / And by disgustful worms was gather'd there." (10-1)

[40] Notice that Beckett read Vico because Joyce asked him. In Beckett's words:

> It was at his [Joyce] suggestion that I wrote "Dante...Bruno.Vico..Joyce"- because of my Italian. I spent a lot of time reading Bruno and Vico in the

magnificent library, the Bibliothèque of the Ecole Normale. We must have had some talk about the "Eternal Return", that sort of thing. He liked the essay. But his only comment on it was that there wasn't enough about Bruno; he found Bruno rather neglected. They were new figures to me at the time. I hadn't read them. I'd worked on Dante, of course. I knew very little of them. I knew more or less what they were about. I remember reading a biography of one of them. (Quoted in Knowlson, 100)

But notice (cf. Peter Hughes and his "From Allusion to Implosion") that Joyce did not read Vico in Italian but through Michelet's "Principles de la philosophie de l'histoire". Beckett directly read Vico's text.

[41] Notice one of Molloy's parodies of Descartes: "For it was not my nature, I mean it was not my custom, to conduct my calculations simultaneously, but separately and turn about, pushing each one as far as it would go before turning in desperation to another." (137)

[42] For the sketch of the Neapolitan situation I refer to Rossi (1993), Reale and Antiseri (1987), Fabietti (1985).

[43] I consider the 1744, definitive, edition of Vico's *Scienza Nuova*.

[44] Cf. Part III for a more careful analyses of the tension contained in *The Unnamable*.

[45] "le cose fuori del loro stato naturale né vi si adagiano né vi durano." (177) But Beckett's unnamable is an example of endurance after having destroyed this "stato naturale".

[46] Moran's trust in Youdi's orders is an example of conforming to what is certain without rationally questioning it.

[47] Cf. Part III, Ch. 1., where I will concentrate on Molloy's instinct.

[48] The problematic of language will be considered later in this chapter.

[49] Notice the etymology of 'theology': Gr. *Theòs* God, and *logia* from *lògos* discourse, and compare it with Beckett's "speaking voice" which gives orders to the characters of the trilogy.

[50] For a careful description of Moran's attitude towards religion cf. Part III, Ch. 1.

[51] But notice that Jacques revolts himself against Moran when they near Ballybaba: once more the presence of Molloy causes an alteration to something that seemed unchangeable.

[52] But notice that Beckett does not neglect the allegorical part, cf. Part 2, Ch. 2 on Dante.

[53] Notice that this impasse remains unresolved throughout Beckett's life: his plays published after *Endgame* concentrate on particulars only.

[54] Notice that Thomas Hunkeler in his *Echos de l'ego dans l'oeuvre de Samuel Beckett* has analysed Beckett's early production, from "Dante...Bruno.Vico..Joyce" (1928-9) to *Watt* (1944). Hunkeler's work is interesting in that it gives

> une possibilité tout a fait prometteuse d'entrer dans l'oeuvre beckettienne par une porte peu remarquée, soigneusement dissimulée aussi, de trouver une voie d'accès à ce qui à ce moment-là n'est pas encore un édifice clos sur lui-même, ou mieux une ruine (dé-)construite de manière méticuleuse, mais un chantier, une oeuvre en construction qui permet des aperçus souvent instructifs pour comprendre l'ouvrage terminé. [...] Toutefois, ce n'est pas tant une biographie de l'oeuvre que *l'émergence d'une poétique* que nous voudrions retracer dans la présente étude. (Hunkeler, 27-33)

[55] It may be interesting to compare them with what Beckett called Proust's "immediate and fortuitous act of perception" (*Proust*, 36), i.e. the remembering caused by an irrelevant action. Molloy's

and Malone's stories seem to be composed of irrelevant actions which fail to activate the act of remembering.

[56] Notice that this sentence is an example of Molloy's dialogue with another part of his conscience. It also shows Molloy's resignation ("I know, I know"), and his desperation ("don't torment me"), an extraordinary strong word for Molloy, usually so neutral in the choice of his vocabulary.

[57] Notice that even Molloy's need to reach his mother is filtered through rationality: "for I must have needed my mother, <u>otherwise why this frenzy of wanting to get to her</u>?" (33, emphasis added).

[58] Notice that Molloy's essence, his mental journey and his linguistic movement could be considered as similar to (and a parody of) Beckett's reflections on the thought of others. In fact, they are all subject to a failing rationality.

[59] Moran's being part of institutions and society (cf. Part 2, Ch. 3., "The Three Ages of Human Society") is further evidence of the exasperation of the rational level.

[60] For a description of what I mean with the <u>Narrator</u> of the trilogy, cf. Part 2, "Dante's Epistola to Cangrande Della Scala".

[61] The only thing Malone remembers is "a mood. My young days were more varied, such as they come back to me, in fits and starts." (169)

[62] Malone's only attempt to move causes a more definite immobility: he tries to displace his bed with his stick in order to "be off and away" (233), but the result he achieves is to lose his stick.

[63] Nor because he is pleased by his style, like Hamm in *Endgame*.

[64] Malone's spiritual journey is similar to that of Molloy and Moran. Notice that it starts and ends inside the character: each one has similar difficulties in understanding and communicating something he feels inside, and finds different solutions. The three narrators have different ways of expressing it, but the force is one and the same.

[65] Malone occasionally tries to react. His attempt to escape from

the room, by moving his bed with the aid of his stick is a desperate attempt to react against his complete immobility.

[66] We have already seen how Malone tries not to notice the presence of the spiritual force, how his rationality escapes from it.

[67] His identification with the other characters of the trilogy is clearly stated. "To tell the truth I believe they are all here, at least from Murphy on, I believe we are all here, but so far I have only seen Malone." (268)

[68] Notice the similarities with Dante's Ante-Inferno, cf. Part 2, "Belacqua and "Colui che fece per viltà il gran rifiuto".

[69] In *The Unnamable* there is a reference to the fact that he is writing, but the unnamable also claims that this is not possible in that he does not feel he possesses any physical part. "How, in such conditions, can I write, to consider only the manual aspect of that bitter folly? I don't know. I could know. But I shall not know. Not this time. It is I who write, who cannot raise my hand from my knee." (276)

[70] Notice that speech is a strong socializing method, and thus the unnamable's words try to bring him back among human beings.

[71] The two stories about Mahood are also, to a certain extent, parodying Molloy's, Moran's, and Malone's accounts. This fact, nevertheless, does not prevent the development of Malone into Mahood because the unnamable is not in total control of Mahood.

[72] In opposition to Mahood. "Can Mahood note? That's it, weave, weave. Yes, it is the characteristic, among others, of Mahood to note, even if he does not always succeed in doing so, certain things, perhaps I should say all things, so as to turn them to account, for his governance." (312)

[73] Note the similarity between the unnamable's words and those spoken to Arjuna by Krishna. "Do thou fight for the sake of fighting, without considering happiness or distress, loss or gain, victory or defeat" (*Bhagavad-Gita*, 122); "Perform your duty equiposed, O Arjuna, abandoning all attachment to success or failure. Such equanimity is called yoga." (136)

[74] As already seen, the unnamable also mentions Watt, Mercier, etc., but I will consider only the characters contained in the trilogy.

[75] And on stories he affirms: "no point in telling yourself stories, to pass the time, stories don't pass the time, nothing passes the time" (354).

[76] Although the episode of cannibalism is not directly stated in the *Divina Commedia*, it is supposed to have happened. "[O]nd'io mi diedi, / già cieco, a brancolar sovra ciascuno," (xxxiii, 72-3) are Ugolino's ambiguous words. Notice the similarity of Conte Ugolino's episode with Molloy: "And all I could see was her taut yellow nape which every now and then I set my teeth in, forgetting I had none, such is the power of instinct." (53-4)

[77] Notice that the unnamable does not consider words and rationality to be connected: "but there it is, I feel nothing, know nothing, and as far as thinking is concerned I do just enough to preserve me from going silent, you can't call that thinking." (281)

[78] The fact that for the unnamable the silence of rationality would be a new beginning shows that he is still unaware of what he wants to express.

[79] Notice that Hamm has, within the play, a double function of character and of actor. This second function enables him to be detached from whatever stands or whoever lives in the shelter. Clov is conscious of that situation and therefore does not emotionally react to Hamm's reciting. But both are aware of Hamm's acting: Clov even claims "Let's stop playing", and Hamm answers "Never!" (77)

[80] This passage is also a joke about the play. A similar joke appears in *The Unnamable*: "It's the end that is the worst, no, it's the beginning that is the worst, then the middle, then the end, in the end it's the end that is the worst, this voice that, I don't know, it's every second that is the worst" (363-4).

[81] That loss of motion and being is noticeable in a descending climax involving the characters: Clov, who can move (more or

less) freely; Hamm, who is trying to; Nagg, who emerges three times from the lid; and Nell, who appears only once and then dies.

[82] Compare it to the dialogue between Molloy and the sergeant (*Molloy*, 22-3).

www.ingramcontent.com/pod-product-compliance
Lightning Source LLC
Chambersburg PA
CBHW020408230426
43664CB00009B/1240